MAIN COURSES

MAIN COURSES

Quick and Easy Vegetarian Dishes

LINDA McCARTNEY AND PETER COX

BLOOMSBURY

To my husband and children who, like me, love animals and enjoy cooking.

Material taken from *Linda McCartney's Home Cooking*, first published 1989

This edition published in 1992
by Bloomsbury Publishing Limited
2 Soho Square, London W1V 5DE

10 9 8 7 6 5 4 3 2

A copy of the CIP entry for this book is available from the British Library.

ISBN 0 7475 1198 5

Designed by Fielding Rowinski
Typeset by Columns of Reading
Printed in Great Britain by Cox & Wyman Ltd., Reading

CONTENTS

Introduction   vii

1. Hot dishes, Pies and Bakes   1

2. Casseroles and Stews   78

3. Vegetable Specialities   104

Index   118

INTRODUCTION

I was lucky enough to grow up in a family of food lovers. We rarely had fancy meals but they always tasted good. I used to spend a lot of time hanging out in the kitchen, partly because I liked to be around food, but also because I loved to watch my mum preparing a meal often without measuring or weighing any ingredients. She just seemed to know instinctively what was right.

I like to think I'm a person who picks things up easily and those hours I spent hanging around the kitchen have served me well. They've given me a natural feeling for putting together a meal without spending hours poring over recipes.

There is, of course, one main difference between my cooking and the food I was brought up on – I don't use any meat but everybody seems to say it tastes as good as, if not better than using (to put it bluntly) dead animals.

Which brings me to the reason I've written this book. Partly as a way of handing down my recipes to my family, but most importantly because I want to encourage all those people who so often say to me: 'I'd like to cook without using meat but I don't know where to begin', or 'How do you fill that gap on the plate where there's usually a piece of lamb or beef?' My response is simple – there are quiches, pastas, salads and many wonderful new soya protein foods that taste so much better than meat!

And to those people who complain: 'I'd love to be a vegetarian but my family would never allow it', I suggest you try a few of my recipes – without mentioning there's no meat – and see how much they enjoy them!

We stopped eating meat many years ago. During the course of a Sunday lunch we happened to look out of the kitchen window at our young lambs gambolling happily in the fields. Glancing down at our plates we suddenly realized that we were eating the leg of an animal that had until recently been gambolling in a field itself. We looked at each other and said 'Wait a minute, we love these sheep – they're such gentle creatures, so why are we eating them?' It was the last time we ever did.

Some people find it easier to cut out meat gradually, supplementing their diet with chicken and fish. We chose not to take this route – a decision which was reinforced a few weeks later when we found ourselves stuck behind a truck packed tightly with beautiful white hens. As it turned into the chicken processing plant a few miles ahead, we imagined the fate in store for those poor hens and felt we had acted wisely.

There are people who try to justify eating fish by saying they have no feelings. Well, you watch a fish gasping for breath as it's pulled out of the water and then try and tell me it has no feelings! Anyway, with the amount of pollution in our poisoned rivers and seas, I'm surprised that *anyone* wants to eat fish. But that's another story. . .

I think a lot of people are rather afraid of cooking. I've met so many people who say: 'Oh, I could never cook that!' when more often than not it's just been a bunch of really good food thrown together – and doesn't it taste good! It's a shame that so many people shy away from the kitchen because it can be an artistic and creative place. And rewarding too – it's great to prepare a meal that is well received.

I don't think you have to be a particularly talented person to be a good cook. It helps enormously, of course, if you enjoy cooking, but even if you don't I hope this book will encourage you to have a go – and maybe you'll find you start to get some unexpected pleasure out of it!

To tell you the truth, I'm a real peasant cook. My cooking has never been about following recipes in a book, and it's been a challenge to translate these instinctive methods into hard and fast rules. For example, if I'm making a stew I *never* weigh the carrots, potatoes, and onions. I simply say: 'that looks the right amount' and in they go. If you like a particular herb, or if you like garlic, onions or potatoes, then add more of what you like to my recipes – don't be afraid to make a few changes to suit your own taste. That's what cooking's all about!

The important thing, I believe, is to have a really good time cooking. Don't be too serious, and – most of all – don't be 'precious'.

I spend a lot of time in our kitchen. I find it the cosiest, friendliest place in the house. It's not something my American upbringing prepared me for, but now that I live in England it's become very important to me. It's a great place to nurture a happy harmonious family and to spend time with friends, chatting over a cup of tea.

I've put down a lot of my favourite recipes here and I really hope you find them as easy to make as I do. They're very popular with everybody I know, and I hope they'll become favourites of yours as well. I haven't written this book in order to be acclaimed as a great cook – like everyone, I've had my share of disasters in the kitchen. I'm simply doing it for the animals.

Linda McCartney

HOT DISHES, PIES and BAKES

Asparagus in Divine Sauce

1½lb/680g asparagus spears
1 onion, chopped
2oz/55g butter or margarine
1oz/25g plain flour
pinch of ground nutmeg (optional)
15fl.oz/430ml vegetable stock or water
2 egg yolks
1 tablespoon lemon juice

to serve:
rice or toast (optional)

Wash and trim the asparagus, then simmer or steam, in batches if necessary, for 4–5 minutes, depending on the thickness of the spears. Drain and cover to keep hot.

Meanwhile, heat the butter in a saucepan and sauté the onion for 4–5 minutes until lightly browned. Sprinkle the flour over the sauté and stir into a thick, smooth paste. Add the nutmeg. Gradually add the vegetable stock and stir continuously to make a smooth sauce. Bring this sauce to the boil, reduce the heat and simmer for 2–3 minutes.

Remove the sauce from the heat. Beat the egg yolks and lemon juice together then gradually add to the sauce, stirring very well after each addition. Place the sauce back on the heat and gently warm through until the sauce begins to thicken again.

Arrange the hot asparagus on a platter (or on a plate of rice, or even on toast) and pour the hot sauce over the spears. Serve immediately.

20 minutes to make

Asparagus with Cheese

Serve with rice or potatoes, and a salad.

1½lb/680g asparagus spears
1oz/25g butter or margarine
2 tablespoons lemon juice
1 lb/455g Gruyère or Emmental cheese, grated
freshly ground black pepper to taste

Pre-heat the oven to 350°F/180°C (Gas Mark 4) and lightly grease a casserole dish. Wash and trim the asparagus, then simmer or steam it, in batches if necessary, for 4–5 minutes depending on the thickness of the spears. Drain well, and arrange it in the casserole dish.

Place small pieces of butter on top of the asparagus and pour the lemon juice over it. Sprinkle the grated cheese over the asparagus and bake for 10 minutes. Season with pepper and serve hot.

25 minutes to make
Good source of protein, vitamin A, B group vitamins, calcium

Aubergine and Pasta

Depending on the size of aubergine you use, this dish should serve 4 very hungry people, or 6 quite hungry ones! Serve with salad or a green vegetable.

3 aubergines
6 tablespoons olive oil
1lb/455g macaroni
1×14oz/397g tin chopped tomatoes
2 tablespoons tomato puree
1 teaspoon dried oregano or 1 tablespoon fresh
1 clove garlic, crushed (optional)
salt and freshly ground black pepper to taste
a little water or vegetable stock
8oz/225g Mozzarella cheese, sliced
1oz/25g butter or margarine
2oz/55g Parmesan cheese, grated

Pre-heat the oven to 350°F/180°C (Gas Mark 4), and lightly grease a casserole dish. Peel the aubergines and slice them lengthways into strips. Heat the oil in a frying pan and brown the aubergine slices on both sides, a few pieces at a time. Use a little more oil if necessary. Remove the slices and place to one side.

Cook the macaroni, following the instructions on the packet, in a large pan of salted water. When cooked, drain thoroughly and return to the large pan.

Add the tomatoes, tomato puree, oregano, garlic and oil from the frying pan to the cooked macaroni. Mix well and season to taste. Add a little water or stock if necessary to make the mixture moist.

Place the aubergine, Mozzarella and macaroni mixture in alternate layers in the casserole dish. Continue until all the ingredients are used.

Place a few dabs of butter over the top layer, sprinkle with Parmesan cheese, and bake uncovered for about 30 minutes, until the top is a bubbling, golden brown.

1 hour to make
Good source of protein, vitamin A, calcium

Aubergine Caponata

This dish is best chilled for 24 hours before serving. Serve with pasta or rice, and a salad.

1 large aubergine
1 small onion
1 stick celery
1oz/25g olives
1oz/25g capers
2½ tablespoons olive oil
1 tablespoon chopped fresh parsley
1 tablespoon wine vinegar
2 teaspoons sugar
1 × 7oz/200g tin chopped tomatoes
1 tablespoon tomato puree

Dice the aubergine into small cubes and sprinkle generously with salt. Leave on a plate for about 20 minutes to draw out the bitterness.

While the aubergine is standing, prepare the rest of the ingredients. Chop the onion, celery, olives and capers into small pieces.

Heat the olive oil in a deep frying pan and sauté the onion and celery for about 5 minutes, until lightly browned. Now wash the salted aubergine thoroughly, drain, and add to the sauté, a few cubes at a time so the pieces do not absorb too much oil. However, add more oil if necessary.

Add the remaining ingredients, cover the pan and simmer, over a medium heat, for 30 minutes.

55 minutes to make
Good source of vitamin C

Aubergine Parmigiano

Serve with pasta or rice, and green vegetables or a salad.

2 aubergines
8–10 tablespoons olive oil
1 medium onion, chopped
2 × 14oz/397g tins chopped tomatoes
1 × 5oz/140g tin tomato puree
1 tablespoon chopped fresh oregano
1 teaspoon chopped fresh basil
3 tablespoons plain flour
8oz/225g Mozzarella cheese, sliced (more to taste)

Pre-heat the oven to 350°F/180°C (Gas Mark 4) and lightly grease a baking dish. Wash the aubergines and slice lengthways into thin strips.

Heat 1 tablespoon of the olive oil in a saucepan and sauté the onion. Add the tinned tomatoes to the sauté, then the tomato puree and the herbs. Stir well and bring this sauce to a simmer. Cover the pan and cook over a low heat for 30 minutes.

Meanwhile, place the flour in a small bowl and dip the aubergine strips into it so that each piece is well coated. Heat the remaining olive oil in a frying pan and sauté the floured aubergine until lightly browned. Add more oil if necessary.

Pour some tomato sauce into the baking dish and place a layer of sautéd aubergine over it. Add another layer of sauce, another of aubergine, and continue in this way until both ingredients are used up. Arrange the cheese slices over the top layer. Bake for 30–40 minutes until the topping is golden brown. Serve immediately.

1 hour 15 minutes to make
Good source of protein, vitamin A, vitamin C, calcium

Baked Macaroni Cheese

Serve with green vegetables or a salad. Delicious any time of year.

12oz/340g macaroni
1 egg
1 pint/570ml milk
1oz/25g butter or margarine
10oz/285g Cheddar cheese, grated
salt and freshly ground black pepper to taste

Pre-heat the oven to 350°F/180°C (Gas Mark 4). Lightly boil the macaroni, for about 5 minutes until half cooked.

Whisk the egg and milk together in a large jug. Melt the butter and add it, with the grated cheese, to the egg and milk. Stir well.

Place the lightly cooked macaroni in a greased baking dish. Pour the egg and cheese liquid over the macaroni, sprinkle with salt and pepper and stir well. Press the mixture evenly around the baking dish. Bake, uncovered, for 30–40 minutes, until the top is brown.

55 minutes to make
Good source of protein, vitamin A, B group vitamins, calcium

Baked Sweetcorn

You can't always get fresh ears of sweetcorn, so do substitute tinned sweetcorn if necessary – it tastes almost as good. Serve with green vegetables or a salad.

1½oz/45g butter or margarine
3 tablespoons plain flour
12fl.oz/340ml cream
1lb/455g sweetcorn kernels (cut from 9–10 ears corn)
3 eggs, beaten
1oz/25g breadcrumbs
salt and freshly ground black pepper to taste

Pre-heat the oven to 350°F/180°C (Gas Mark 4) and lightly grease a casserole dish. Melt 1oz/25g of the butter in a saucepan and sprinkle the flour over it. Stir constantly over the heat to make a thick paste.

Heat the cream in another saucepan, then add it very gradually to the paste, stirring after each addition to make a smooth sauce. Remove from the heat.

Add the corn and eggs to the sauce and stir well.

Melt the remaining butter in a deep saucepan and stir in the breadcrumbs, salt and pepper. Pour the corn mixture into the casserole, cover with the breadcrumbs and place the casserole in a baking tray filled with hot water. Bake, uncovered, for 25–30 minutes. Serve immediately.

45 minutes to make
Good source of protein, vitamin A

Beefless Pie

It may be called 'Beefless', but it really does have all the flavour and texture of beef, particularly if you buy beef-flavoured TVP chunks. Vegetable suet or shortening is easy to buy in any supermarket. Serve this pie with vegetables or a salad.

> 2oz/55g vegetable suet
> 1 large onion
> 1 × 4½oz/128g packet TVP chunks, or 4 vegetable
>   burgers, cubed
> 1 clove garlic, crushed
> 16fl.oz/460ml vegetable stock or water (8fl.oz if using
>   vegetable burgers)
> 1 tablespoon soy sauce
> 1 bay leaf
> 1 teaspoon mixed herbs
> salt and freshly ground black pepper to taste
> 2 tablespoons plain flour
> 6oz/170g shortcrust pastry

Pre-heat the oven to 425°F/220°C (Gas Mark 7). Melt the vegetable suet in a large saucepan. Chop the onion and place it in the hot fat with the TVP chunks and garlic. Sauté until the onion and garlic are lightly browned, stirring often.

Stir in the vegetable stock, soy sauce, bay leaf and mixed herbs. Cover the mixture and simmer for 20 minutes, until the chunks are tender.

Mix the flour with a little vegetable stock to make a smooth solution, and stir this into the dish after it has simmered for 15 minutes, to thicken the sauce.

Roll out the pastry to fit the top of a casserole dish.   Transfer the TVP mixture into the casserole dish and cover with the pastry. Prick the pastry lid in several places with a fork, and place the pie in the hot oven.

After 10 minutes, reduce the heat of the oven to 350°F/180°C (Gas Mark 4) and bake for a further 20 minutes.

55 minutes to make
Good source of protein

Beer Fondue

Serve with sautéd mushrooms and greens, or new potatoes and a salad.

8 slices bread
1–2oz/25–55g butter or margarine
4oz/115g Swiss or Cheddar cheese, sliced
3 eggs
1 teaspoon soy sauce
½ teaspoon mild mustard
½ pint/290ml beer
salt and freshly ground black pepper to taste

Pre-heat the oven to 350°F/180°C (Gas Mark 4) and lightly oil a large casserole dish. Remove the crusts from the slices of bread and lightly butter them on both sides.

Arrange the bread and cheese slices in alternate layers in the casserole dish.

Beat the remaining ingredients together in a jug. Pour this mixture over the bread and cheese layers, pressing the bread down well with a wooden spoon.

Bake the casserole, uncovered, for 30 minutes. Serve immediately.

40 minutes to make
Good source of protein, B group vitamins, calcium

Cauliflower Mexican Style

Serve with a selection of steamed vegetables. For a spicier variation, substitute the capers, cloves and cinnamon with 1×4oz/115g tin green chillies, drained and finely chopped.

1 large cauliflower
15fl.oz/430ml home-made tomato sauce
1 tablespoon capers
2 tablespoons chopped onion
3 tablespoons chopped fresh parsley
large pinch of ground cloves
large pinch of ground cinnamon
salt and freshly ground black pepper to taste
3 tablespoons breadcrumbs
8oz/225g Cheddar cheese, grated

Pre-heat the oven to 400°F/200°C (Gas Mark 6) and lightly grease a casserole dish. Cut the cauliflower into florets and steam or simmer until tender, then drain.

Place the cauliflower florets in a large mixing bowl, add the tomato sauce, capers, onion, parsley, cloves, cinnamon, salt and pepper and mix well. Pour the mixture into the casserole dish.

Mix the breadcrumbs and cheese together in a separate bowl, then sprinkle them over the casserole.

Bake, uncovered, for 30 minutes, until the topping is golden brown. Serve immediately.

1 hour to make
Good source of protein, vitamin A, vitamin C, calcium

Cheddar Cheese Bake

Serve hot with spinach or green vegetables and salad.

1 tablespoon olive oil
2 cloves garlic, crushed
8oz/225g Cheddar cheese, sliced thinly
3 eggs, beaten
1oz/25g plain flour
12fl.oz/340ml milk
4fl.oz/120ml single cream
salt and freshly ground black pepper to taste

Pre-heat the oven to 375°F/190°C (Gas Mark 5). Heat the oil in a small frying pan and sauté the garlic. Pour the sauté into a casserole dish.

Place half the cheese in the baking dish and spread to cover the bottom. Combine the remaining ingredients and pour over the cheese in the casserole dish.

Top the dish with the remaining Cheddar slices and bake, uncovered, for 30 minutes. Serve immediately.

40 minutes to make
Good source of protein, vitamin A, B group vitamins, calcium

Cheddar Cheese Pie

This is as tasty cold as it is hot. Serve with greens, carrots or a salad.

6oz/170g shortcrust pastry (enough to line your pie dish)
3 eggs, beaten
1 medium onion, chopped
1oz/25g butter or margarine
8fl.oz/230ml double cream
8oz/225g Cheddar cheese, grated
salt and freshly ground black pepper to taste

Pre-heat the oven to 400°F/200°C (Gas Mark 6). Grease a 9 inch/23cm pie dish, then line it with the pastry and flute the edges. Brush a little beaten egg on the pastry and bake it blind for about 10 minutes. Remove from the oven, and reduce the oven heat to 375°F/190°C (Gas Mark 5).

Sauté the onion in the butter for 4–5 minutes or until golden brown, and spread the mixture on to the cooked pastry. Mix the cream, grated cheese and seasoning in with the remaining beaten egg. Pour this mixture into the pie crust.

Bake for 30 minutes until the crust is nicely browned and the filling firmly set.

50 minutes to make
Good source of vitamin A, B group vitamins, calcium

Cheese Soufflé

It helps to have an electric blender for this recipe, because it will save you a lot of effort! Don't be intimidated by soufflés – once you've got the hang of them they're easy to make, and always go down well. My kids make great soufflés! For a tasty variation on this recipe, finely chop some fresh tarragon into the soufflé mixture.

1oz/25g butter or margarine
1oz/25g plain flour
½ pint/290ml milk
salt and freshly ground black pepper to taste
4oz/115g Cheddar cheese, grated
4 eggs, separated

Pre-heat the oven to 375°F/190°C (Gas Mark 5). Grease a 1 pint/570ml soufflé dish. Melt the butter in a saucepan then add the flour, whisking to a smooth paste. Cook for 1 minute over a low heat.

Heat the milk in a separate pan and add it gradually to the flour paste, stirring constantly. When all the milk is added, simmer the sauce for 2–3 minutes, stirring occasionally. Season to taste. Remove from the heat and allow to cool for 2 minutes.

Now add the grated cheese, and stir the mixture, off the heat, until the cheese has melted. Beat the egg yolks, add to the cheese mixture and stir until well blended.

In another bowl, whisk the egg whites until they are stiff but not dry. Then fold them carefully into the cheese mixture. Turn the whole mixture into the soufflé dish and bake for 30–35 minutes. Serve immediately.

50 minutes to make
Good source of protein, vitamin A, B group vitamins, calcium

Cheese with Herbs and Pasta

1oz/25g butter or margarine
1 large onion, chopped
3 cloves garlic, crushed
1lb/455g small pasta (e.g. macaroni or pasta shells)
7fl.oz/205ml sour cream
1lb/455g ricotta or cottage cheese
2 tablespoons chopped fresh parsley or 1 tablespoon dried
4 tablespoons chopped fresh basil or 1 tablespoon dried
2 tablespoons chopped fresh oregano or 1 tablespoon dried
salt and freshly ground black pepper to taste
1 tablespoon grated Parmesan cheese

Melt the butter in a large frying pan and gently sauté the onion and garlic until tender, about 5 minutes. Set the pasta to cook in boiling water.

Mix the sour cream and ricotta cheese to a smooth consistency. Add the parsley, basil and oregano and stir well. Season with the salt and pepper. Add this mixture to the sauté and place over a very low heat, stirring frequently.

When the pasta has cooked, drain and rinse it well. Turn it into a serving dish and stir in the hot cheese sauce. Serve immediately, sprinkled with a little grated Parmesan.

35 minutes to make
Good source of protein, vitamin A, B group vitamins, vitamin C

Corn Soufflé

Serve with a selection of vegetables or a salad.

1oz/25g butter or margarine
1 teaspoon salt
¼ teaspoon freshly ground black pepper
1oz/25g plain flour
8fl.oz/230ml milk
8oz/225g sweetcorn kernels, cooked and drained
4 eggs, separated

Pre-heat the oven to 375°F/190°C (Gas Mark 5) and lightly grease a 1 pint/570ml soufflé dish. Melt the butter in a saucepan. Stir the salt and pepper into the flour, then sprinkle the flour over the hot butter. Stir well to make a thick paste.

Gradually add the milk to the paste, stirring after each addition, to make a smooth white sauce. Simmer for 2 minutes, then remove the saucepan from the heat.

Add the sweetcorn to the white sauce and stir well. Remove the sauce from the heat and allow to cool briefly. Then stir the egg yolks into the sauce.

Beat the egg whites until they are very stiff, then fold them gently into the corn and white sauce mixture. Turn the mixture into the soufflé dish and bake, undisturbed, for 30 minutes. Serve immediately.

45 minutes to make
Good source of protein, B group vitamins

Cottage Cheese Pie

Serve with a salad, steamed vegetables or grilled tomatoes and a sauce or relish.

6oz/170g shortcrust pastry (enough to line a 9 inch/ 23cm pie dish)
1¼lb/570g potatoes
4oz/115g cottage cheese
2fl.oz/60ml sour cream
2 tablespoons chopped chives
1 tablespoon chopped tarragon
salt and freshly ground black pepper to taste
½oz/15g butter or margarine

Pre-heat the oven to 400°F/200°C (Gas Mark 6). Grease the pie dish, then roll out the pastry to line it. Flute the edges and bake blind for 10 minutes. When you remove the pie dish from the oven reduce the oven temperature to 350°F/180°C (Gas Mark 4).

Boil the potatoes and mash them, while still hot, with the cottage cheese, sour cream and herbs. Season to taste.

Spoon this mixture into the pie shell, spread it evenly and dot with small pieces of the butter. Bake for 20–25 minutes or until the filling is nicely browned on top and the pastry has finished cooking. If the top becomes too brown, cover with foil. Serve immediately.

1 hour to make
Good source of protein, vitamin A, B group vitamins, vitamin C

Curried Lentils

2 tablespoons olive oil
2 medium onions, chopped
2 cloves garlic, crushed
1–2 tablespoons curry powder (or to taste)
1 teaspoon ground cumin
8oz/225g lentils
1 pint/570ml vegetable stock or water
2 tablespoons lemon juice
½ tablespoon grated lemon rind
salt and freshly ground black pepper to taste

Heat the oil in a deep saucepan and sauté the onions for 4–5 minutes. Add the garlic and spices and cook for 2 minutes. Wash, rinse and drain the lentils and add them to the sauté. Cook for a further 2 minutes.

Pour the stock into the pan, and add the lemon juice and rind. Bring to the boil, then season to taste. Cover, reduce the heat and simmer for 20–25 minutes, stirring occasionally. Add a little extra stock if necessary. The lentils should be quite soft when cooked. Serve hot.

45 minutes to make
Good source of protein, vitamin C, iron

Eggs au Gratin

15fl.oz/430ml white sauce
6 eggs
1 tablespoon chopped chives
4oz/115g Cheddar cheese, grated
1oz/25g breadcrumbs

Pre-heat the oven to 350°F/180°C (Gas Mark 4) and lightly grease a casserole dish.

Prepare the white sauce and keep warm over a low heat. Hard-boil the eggs and, when cool enough to handle, peel and slice them.

Line the casserole dish with the hard-boiled eggs. Sprinkle the chopped chives over the eggs and spread half the grated cheese over the chives.

Pour the white sauce over the eggs and cheese and sprinkle the remaining grated cheese over the sauce. Top the casserole with the breadcrumbs and bake for about 15–20 minutes, until golden brown. Serve immediately.

30 minutes to make
Good source of protein, B group vitamins, calcium

Eggs Florentine

1½lb/680g spinach
2oz/55g butter or margarine
1oz/25g plain flour
¼ teaspoon ground nutmeg
salt and freshly ground black pepper to taste
6 eggs
5fl.oz/140ml milk
5fl.oz/140ml cream
2oz/55g Cheddar cheese

Pre-heat the oven to 400°F/200°C (Gas Mark 6) and lightly grease an oven dish. Wash and trim the spinach then place it in a deep saucepan over a high heat. Do not add any water. Cover the pan and leave to cook for 2 minutes, then reduce the heat and cook for a further 5 minutes. Remove the pan from the heat, allow the spinach to cool slightly, and then puree it in a blender.

Melt half of the butter in a saucepan, sprinkle half of the flour over it and stir well. Add the spinach puree and cook for 2–3 minutes, then season well with nutmeg, salt and pepper. Spoon the puree into a shallow oven dish. Poach the eggs and place them over the puree.

Melt the remaining butter, and stir the remaining flour into it, then gradually add the milk and cream and bring to simmering point. Cook for 3 minutes. Then remove from the heat, stir in the grated cheese and pour the sauce over the poached eggs. Bake for 10–15 minutes, until the cheese topping is a golden brown.

45 minutes to make
Good source of protein, vitamin A, B group vitamins, vitamin C

Festive or Sunday Roast with Savoury Stuffing

'But what do you eat for Christmas dinner?' is the usual question friends ask us when they hear we don't eat meat. Well, here it is! It may take a little time to prepare, but even so, it's still much less hassle than wrestling with a dead turkey on Christmas day! And it's *so* much tastier too. Decorate the table with holly, Christmas bowls, and crackers, and you can really enjoy a traditional Christmas dinner – in fact the only thing missing is the cruelty! Like us, you'll probably find that you will want to use this recipe for other occasions, such as birthdays, New Year's Eve, Easter, Guy Fawkes Night, and dinner parties.

2 tablespoons garlic powder
12oz/340g vegetable sausage mix
1 egg
4 vegetable schnitzels or 5 vegetable burgers
1 × 4½oz/128g packet TVP mince, unflavoured
4 tablespoons soy sauce or vegetable extract
3 tablespoons vegetable oil

Start preparing the roast the day before it is needed. Pre-heat the oven to 180°C/350°F (Gas Mark 4). Grease and flour a large casserole dish or mould. Sprinkle 1 tablespoon of the garlic powder all over the inside of this dish.

Measure the sausage mix, egg, and 1 pint/570ml water into a large mixing bowl. Stir well and leave for 5 minutes for the liquid to be absorbed.

Measure ¼ pint/140ml water into a food blender. Add the vegetable burgers and blend to an even consistency.

Mix the TVP mince and 1 pint/570ml of water in a bowl. Stir well and leave to stand for 5 minutes.

Combine the sausage mix, pureed burgers and the soaked TVP mince together in a large bowl. Add the remaining garlic powder and the soy sauce. Mix well. Coat the casserole dish with the vegetable oil, and pour the mixture into the dish, pressing it firmly on to the sides and bottom. Leave a large cavity in the middle for the stuffing. Firm the mixture with the back of a spoon or your knuckles.

Bake for 1½ hours in the hot oven. Allow to cool, then cover and place overnight in the refrigerator.

The next day, make the savoury stuffing.

Savoury Stuffing

1 loaf brown bread, cubed
6 tablespoons margarine
5 stalks celery, chopped
1 large onion, chopped
4 fresh sage leaves, finely chopped
1 tablespoon mixed dried herbs

Pre-heat the oven to 180°C/350°F (Gas Mark 4).

Place the cubes of brown bread in a large mixing bowl. Melt the margarine in a large frying pan. Add the celery and onion and, stirring frequently with a wooden spoon, sauté for 5 minutes, until lightly brown.

Pour the sauté into the mixing bowl with the bread cubes. Add ½ pint/285ml water, the sage and the mixed herbs. Mix very well and use.

10 minutes to make

Fill the roast cavity with this stuffing. Any remainder may be placed in a baking dish and baked separately later.

Turn the casserole dish upside down on to a baking tray or roasting pan without removing the dish, place in the oven and bake for 45 minutes. Remove the casserole dish and continue to bake for 1 more hour. After half an hour, place the extra stuffing in the oven and bake for the remaining 30 minutes.

Serve the stuffed roast hot with gravy, the extra stuffing, and side dishes of baked sweet potatoes, cranberry sauce, mashed and roast potatoes, onions and parsnips, steamed Brussels sprouts and green peas.

1 hour 50 minutes, plus 2 hours to make
Good source of protein, calcium, potassium, iron, zinc.

French Baked Eggs

Serve on a bed of rice or with a green salad.

  6 *large tomatoes*
  2 *cloves garlic, crushed*
  2 *tablespoons chopped fresh parsley*
  salt and freshly ground black pepper to taste
  6 *eggs*
  4 *tablespoons grated Parmesan cheese*

Pre-heat the oven to 350°F/180°C (Gas Mark 4) and lightly grease a baking dish. Slice the tops off the tomatoes, scoop out their centres and discard the pulp. Arrange the tomato shells in the baking dish.

Mix the garlic and parsley together in a small bowl. Season to taste. Spoon equal amounts into the tomato shells. Bake for 5–6 minutes.

Remove the tomatoes from the oven and break one egg into the centre of each. Return to the oven and bake for a further 10 minutes, until the eggs are well cooked.

Sprinkle the eggs with a little Parmesan and brown under a hot grill if desired. Serve immediately.

20 minutes to make
Good source of protein, vitamin A, B group vitamins, vitamin C

Baked Macaroni Cheese (p. 6)

Aubergine Parmigiano (p. 5)

Burgers Bourguignonne (p. 85)

Cauliflower Mexican Style (p. 10)

Gnocchi

Unlike most of the other recipes, this is a dish that requires a fair amount of skill – but persevere and you'll get it right!

1lb/455g potatoes
2 egg yolks
salt and freshly ground black pepper to taste
4oz/115g plain flour, plus a little sprinkling flour
12fl.oz/340ml Home-made Tomato Sauce (see page 147)
3–4 tablespoons grated Parmesan cheese

Scrub the potatoes and boil them in their jackets. When tender, peel them and mash in a mixing bowl.

Add the egg yolks and seasoning and beat the mixture until it is light and fluffy. Add the flour and mix well. Turn out on to a floured board and knead lightly, adding more flour if necessary to make a very smooth dough.

Divide the dough into 6 parts. Use your hands to roll each part on a lightly-floured board to make a long sausage shape, about 1¼ inches/3cm in diameter. Cut each roll into 1 inch/2cm lengths, indent them with a fork and sprinkle lightly with flour.

Bring a large saucepan of water to the boil and drop the gnocchi pieces into it. Boil about 12–15 at a time for 2–3 minutes or until they float to the surface. Remove and drain.

In a separate saucepan, heat the tomato sauce. Place the gnocchi on a serving plate, cover with the hot tomato sauce and sprinkle with Parmesan cheese.

1 hour to make
Good source of vitamin A, B Group vitamins, vitamin C, potassium

Green Chilli and Rice

8oz/225g long grain rice
1×4oz/115g tin green chillies in brine
8oz/225g Cheddar cheese, grated
8fl.oz/230ml sour cream
1 tablespoon cornflour
salt and freshly ground black pepper to taste
1oz/25g butter or margarine

Pre-heat the oven to 350°F/180°C (Gas Mark 4) and lightly grease a baking dish. If necessary, wash the rice in cold water once or twice, then drain. Cover the rice with twice its volume of water (i.e. 1 cup rice to 2 cups water) in a medium-sized saucepan. Bring to a boil, then cover the pan, reduce the heat and leave the rice to simmer for about 20 minutes or until all the water is absorbed.

Drain and chop the chillies. When the rice has finished cooking, stir in the chopped chillies and half the grated cheese. Mix the sour cream with the cornflour and add to the rice. Season to taste.

Transfer the rice mixture into a greased baking dish and dab small pieces of butter on top. Sprinkle the remaining Cheddar over the dish and bake for 15 minutes, uncovered, until the cheese is brown and bubbly.

45 minutes to make
Good source of vitamin A, vitamin C, calcium

Hearts of Artichoke with Mushroom Sauce

Serve hot with rice, vegetables and a side salad.

4 large globe artichokes
1oz/25g butter or margarine
4oz/115g mushrooms, finely diced
salt and freshly ground black pepper to taste
1 tablespoon chopped fresh tarragon
1 egg yolk
4fl.oz/120ml cream
2 tablespoons lemon juice

Bring a large pot of water to the boil. Remove the stems, outer leaves and the top quarter of each artichoke and place them in the boiling water so that the hearts are covered. Simmer for 30 minutes or until tender.

Heat the butter in a frying pan and add the chopped mushrooms. Cook for 3–4 minutes, stirring constantly. Add the salt, pepper and tarragon and continue stirring.

Whisk the egg yolk in a small bowl. Add the cream and mix well. Then add the lemon juice and whisk together. Add this sauce to the mushrooms and stir constantly over a low heat. Do not allow the sauce to boil.

When the artichokes are tender, remove their remaining leaves and the prickly 'choke' from the centre. Discard the chokes and place the hot hearts on a warm serving dish. Spoon the mushroom sauce over them and serve immediately.

45 minutes to make
Good source of vitamin A, B group vitamins, vitamin C, iron

Herby Cheese and Rice Bowl

8oz/225g white rice
2 tablespoons olive oil
3 tablespoons chopped fresh basil or parsley or a mixture of the two or 1
tablespoon dried herbs
6oz/170g Mozzarella cheese, chopped
2–3 tablespoons grated Parmesan cheese

If necessary, wash the rice in cold water once or twice, then drain. Cover the rice with twice its volume of water (1 cup rice to 2 cups water) in a medium-sized saucepan. Bring to a boil, then cover the pan, reduce the heat and leave the rice to simmer for about 20 minutes or until all the water is absorbed.

Empty the rice into a large bowl and stir in the olive oil and herbs. Stir the Mozzarella into the hot rice – the Mozzarella must melt. Sprinkle the Parmesan over the top of the dish and serve immediately.

30 minutes to make
Good source of protein, vitamin A, calcium, iron

Hot Dogs and Tomatoes

This German dish is great accompanied with Sauerkraut (see page 117) and mashed or boiled potatoes, or potato pancakes.

2 tablespoons vegetable oil
2 cloves garlic, crushed
2 large onions, chopped
1 green pepper, deseeded and chopped
1 tablespoon caraway seeds
2 × 14oz/397g tins chopped tomatoes
1 tablespoon paprika
8–12 (depending on size) vegetable frankfurters or bangers
salt and freshly ground black pepper to taste

Heat the oil in a large saucepan and sauté the garlic and onions over a medium heat.

Add the chopped green pepper, cover the sauce-pan, reduce the heat and cook for 10 minutes, stirring occasionally.

Stir in the caraway seeds, tomatoes and paprika. Cover again, and simmer for a further 20 minutes.

Add the vegetable frankfurters and allow to cook for 3–5 minutes. Add the seasoning, stir well and cook for 10 minutes.

50 minutes to make
Good source of vitamin A, vitamin C

Lasagne Italiano

Serve with a salad or green vegetables. Serves 6.

4 tablespoons olive oil
2 cloves garlic, crushed
1 medium onion, chopped
2 sticks celery, chopped
2 × 14oz/397g tins chopped tomatoes
1 × 5oz/140g tin tomato puree
8 tablespoons tomato juice
¼ teaspoon sugar
salt and freshly ground black pepper to taste
12–15 sheets lasagne
8oz/225g Mozzarella cheese, finely chopped

Pre-heat the oven to 350°F/180°C (Gas Mark 4) and lightly grease a deep casserole dish. Heat the oil in a saucepan and sauté the garlic and onion until soft and golden. Add the celery, tomatoes, tomato puree, tomato juice, sugar, salt and pepper. Stir well, cover the pan and simmer gently for 45 minutes.

Cook the lasagne in boiling water following the manufacturer's instructions, until it just begins to soften. Drain, and cover with cold water until needed.

Arrange the lasagne layers in the casserole dish: pasta, sauce, Mozzarella. Repeat these layers until all the ingredients are used.

Top the dish with a layer of cheese and bake for 30 minutes. Cut into portions and serve immediately.

1 hour 30 minutes to make
Good source of protein, vitamin A, vitamin C, calcium

Lentil Cheese Loaf

Serve with a vegetarian gravy, tomato sauce or cheese sauce and a green salad.

6oz/170g lentils
4oz/115g Cheddar cheese, grated
1 onion, chopped
salt and freshly ground black pepper to taste
1 teaspoon dried herb (rosemary or sage or thyme)
2oz/55g fresh breadcrumbs
1 egg, beaten
1½oz/45g butter or margarine

Pre-heat the oven to 350°F/180°C (Gas Mark 4) and lightly grease a 1lb/455g loaf tin. Wash the lentils twice in cold water and drain them well. Cover them with twice their volume of cold water in a large saucepan, cover and bring to a boil. Reduce the heat and simmer the lentils for 20 minutes, until they are quite soft.

Mix the cheese, onion, salt, pepper and herbs in with the cooked lentils.

Add the breadcrumbs, egg and butter to the lentil mixture and stir well. Add more breadcrumbs if the mixture is sloppy.

Press the mixture into the loaf tin and bake for 40–45 minutes. Turn out on to a platter and serve hot.

1 hour 15 minutes to make
Good source of protein, calcium

Linda's Lasagne

This is rather more filling than the Lasagne Italiano recipe above, and a little more special. Avoid using a thick, heavy pasta or you'll find the whole dish becomes stodgy. It will keep well in the fridge or freezer – just cover it when reheating to avoid drying the pasta. This makes enough for 6 people – serve hot with a side salad.

12–15 strips lasagne
4 tablespoons olive oil
1 large onion, chopped
2 cloves garlic, crushed
half a 4½oz/128g packet TVP mince
3 × 14oz/397g tins chopped tomatoes
1 teaspoon dried oregano
salt and freshly ground black pepper to taste
a little vegetable stock or water
8oz/225g cottage cheese
8oz/225g Cheddar cheese, grated

Pre-heat the oven to 350°F/180°C (Gas Mark 4). Place the lasagne strips in a saucepan, cover with water and boil for a few minutes until they are just starting to soften (most brands advise you to do this, but check the instructions on the packet).

Heat the oil in a large saucepan and sauté the onion and garlic. Then add the TVP mince, chopped tomatoes with their juice, oregano, salt and pepper. Simmer for 20–30 minutes, adding a little stock or water if necessary to make a moist sauce. Remove from the heat.

Pour a layer of tomato sauce into a large, deep baking dish. Spoon a layer of cottage cheese over the sauce, then arrange a layer of lasagne over that, followed by a layer of grated Cheddar. Repeat this layering process until you're about 1½ inches/4cm away from the top of the baking dish. Finish with a layer of tomato sauce topped by a final layer of Cheddar cheese.

Bake the lasagne for 30 minutes, until the cheese is brown and bubbly.

1 hour 10 minutes to make
Good source of protein, B group vitamins, calcium, iron

Maine Sauerkraut

Serve with veggy hot dogs and noodles.

2lb/910g fresh sauerkraut (see recipe on page 117)
1 apple
2 tablespoons vegetable oil
1 medium onion, chopped
half a 4½oz/128g packet TVP chunks (or 2 vegetable burgers, cubed)
1 large potato, grated
1 tablespoon caraway seeds
1 pint/570ml. water

Prepare the sauerkraut. Peel, core and slice the apple.

Heat the oil in a deep saucepan and sauté the onion until it is lightly browned. Add the TVP chunks and sauté for a further 5 minutes, stirring often.

Add the potato and caraway to the pan and cover with the water. Bring to the boil, then simmer, covered, for 1 hour over a low heat. Stir occasion-ally, adding extra water if necessary.

1 hour 10 minutes to make
Good source of vitamin C, iron

Meatless Loaf

This recipe is an all-time favourite with me and with just about everyone who tries it (usually the main complaint is that there's never enough). I serve it with any green vegetable (such as gently steamed broccoli, spinach or French beans), and a helping of mashed potatoes, boiled rice or pasta. A green salad is a good starter or accompaniment.

2 tablespoons sunflower oil
2 medium onions, chopped
2 × 4½oz/128g packet TVP mince
10fl.oz/340ml hot water or vegetable stock
3oz/85g breadcrumbs
½ tablespoon mixed herbs
1 tablespoon freshly chopped parsley
2 cloves garlic, crushed or 1 teaspoon garlic powder
1 egg, beaten
5fl.oz/140ml sour cream
2 tablespoons soy sauce
salt and freshly ground black pepper to taste

for the sauce:
2 × 14oz/397g tins chopped tomatoes
1 × 5oz/140g tin tomato puree
salt and freshly ground black pepper to taste

Pre-heat the oven to 350°F/180°C (Gas Mark 4). Heat the oil in a large saucepan and sauté the onions until lightly browned. Add the TVP mince, stir and cook for 2 minutes. Pour the hot water or stock over the sauté and simmer for 4 minutes.

In a separate bowl, mix the breadcrumbs, herbs and garlic together with ½ pint/290ml cold water. Stir in the egg and leave to one side for 10 minutes.

Combine the cooked TVP mince with the bread-crumb mixture, then add the sour cream and soy sauce. Stir well and season to taste.

Using your hands, shape the mixture into an oval mound and place it in the centre of a large baking dish, leaving plenty of space all round for the tomato sauce to run.

Heat the tomatoes, tomato puree and seasoning in a small saucepan, and pour over the loaf, then bake for 1 hour.

1 hour 20 minutes to make
Good source of protein, vitamin A, vitamin C, potassium

Meatless Loaf with Herbs

1½oz/45g fresh breadcrumbs
6oz/170g vegetable sausage mix
salt and freshly ground black pepper to taste
1 teaspoon sweet dried herb mixture (sage, rosemary, thyme)
1 tablespoon chopped fresh parsley
2 eggs, beaten
½ pint/290ml cold water
½oz/15g butter or margarine
1 medium onion, chopped
1 × 4½oz/128g packet TVP mince
12fl.oz/340ml tomato juice

Pre-heat the oven to 325°F/170°C/(Gas Mark 3). Mix the breadcrumbs, sausage mix, salt, pepper, dried herbs, parsley, eggs and water together in a mixing bowl. Stir very well and leave the mixture to one side.

Melt the butter in a frying pan. Sauté the onion for about 5 minutes until lightly browned. Add the TVP mince and continue to sauté for 1–2 minutes, then add the tomato juice, stir and simmer for 10 minutes.

Stir the contents of the frying pan into the sausage mixture in the bowl.

Press into a greased and lined 2lb/910g loaf tin and bake for 1 hour.

1 hour 20 minutes to make
Good source of vitamin A, vitamin C

Mexican Corn Pudding

You can substitute carrots, potatoes, onions or any other vegetable (or combination) for corn in this recipe – experiment for yourself!

> *6 ears sweetcorn or 2 × 12oz/340g tins sweetcorn, drained*
> *1 pint/570ml milk*
> *2 eggs, beaten*
> *1 × 4oz/115g tin green chillies in brine*
> *salt and freshly ground black pepper to taste*
> *1oz/25g butter or margarine*

Pre-heat the oven to 350°F/180°C (Gas Mark 4). Slice all the corn kernels away from the raw cob.

Warm the milk and stir the corn and eggs into it. Drain, rinse and chop the chillies. Add them, with the salt and pepper, to the corn mixture.

Dab a baking dish with the butter and pour the pudding mixture into it. Place this inside a larger dish filled with water, then put them both into the hot oven.

Bake for 30–40 minutes, until a single piece of uncooked spaghetti inserted into the pudding comes out clean.

50 minutes to make
Good source of vitamin A, B group vitamins, vitamin C, calcium

Mexican Loaf

This recipe fills two 2lb/910g loaf tins, and should serve 6–8 people. To make 16fl.oz/460ml tomato sauce, sauté 1 onion in 1 tablespoon olive oil. Add 1 × 14oz/397g tin of tomatoes, chopped, 1 tablespoon tomato puree and 1 teaspoon dried basil and 1 clove crushed garlic. Simmer for 15–20 minutes.

> *1oz/25g butter or margarine*
> *1 clove garlic, crushed*
> *4 vegetable burgers, crumbled, or 1 × 4½oz/128g packet TVP chunks*
> *8oz/225g fresh sweetcorn or 1 × 12oz/340g tin sweetcorn 1 × 4oz/115g*
> *tin green chillies in brine, drained and chopped*
> *½ teaspoon chilli powder*
> *salt and freshly ground black pepper to taste*
> *8fl.oz/230ml cold tomato sauce (double this if using TVP chunks instead of*
> *burgers)*
> *5oz/140g corn meal*
> *2 eggs*

Pre-heat the oven to 350°F/180°C (Gas Mark 4) and lightly grease two 2lb/910g loaf tins. Melt the butter in a large frying pan and sauté the garlic. Crumble the burgers into the sauté and stir well.

Slice the corn off the raw cob. Add the corn, chillies, chilli powder, salt and pepper to the sauté and stir well.

In a separate bowl, whisk the tomato sauce, corn meal and eggs to a smooth consistency. Add this to the mixture in the pan and remove from the heat.

Stir the mixture well, then spoon into the prepared tins. Place the tins in a large tray of water and bake for 1 hour.

1 hour 15 minutes to make
Good source of protein, vitamin A, vitamin C

Moussaka

This famous Greek dish is, in my opinion, even better for using TVP mince. You can eat it straight from the oven, with greens such as broccoli or spinach, but I really prefer the flavour when it's been allowed to cool for at least 6 hours and then reheated. It keeps very well in the fridge or freezer.

3 medium aubergines
6–8 tablespoons olive oil
2 onions, chopped
half a 4½oz/128g packet TVP mince or 2 vegetable burgers, cubed
½ pint/290ml red wine
½ pint/290ml vegetable stock (¼ pint if using vegetable burgers)
4 tablespoons chopped fresh parsley
¼ teaspoon ground cinnamon
¼ teaspoon ground nutmeg
salt and freshly ground black pepper to taste
3 tablespoons tomato puree

for the sauce:
1½oz/45g butter or margarine
1oz/25g plain flour
15fl.oz/430ml milk
2 eggs, beaten
8oz/225g cottage cheese
2oz/55g breadcrumbs
4oz/115g Parmesan cheese

Pre-heat the oven to 375°F/190°C (Gas Mark 5) and grease a large (12 × 18 inches/30cm × 45cm) baking tray. Peel the aubergines and slice into ½ inch/1–2cm strips. Heat 4–6 tablespoons of the oil in a frying pan and brown the aubergine strips on both sides, then remove them from the pan and set them aside. Add more oil if necessary and sauté the onions.

Add the TVP mince to the frying pan and sauté for 5 minutes. Add the red wine, stock, parsley, cinnamon, nutmeg, salt, pepper and tomato puree. Simmer this mixture over a low heat, uncovered, for about 15 minutes until most of the liquid has been absorbed. Remove from the heat and set aside.

Make a white sauce – melt the butter and sprinkle the flour over it. Stir into a smooth, thick paste. Heat the milk and slowly add it to the paste, stirring well after each addition to make a smooth sauce. Remove the sauce from the heat, leave to cool, then stir in the eggs and cottage cheese.

Sprinkle some breadcrumbs evenly over the baking tray. Place a layer of aubergine over the breadcrumbs, cover them with a layer of the TVP mince in sauce, then sprinkle with a thin layer of Parmesan cheese. Repeat the layering process, starting with the breadcrumbs, until the aubergine strips have been used up. Pour the cheese sauce over the dish and top with more Parmesan cheese. Bake for 40–50 minutes, until the cheese turns golden brown.

1 hour 35 minutes to make
Good source of protein, vitamin A, B group vitamins, calcium

Mushroom Loaf

Serve with a fresh green salad or green vegetables or pasta.

2oz/55g breadcrumbs
8fl.oz/230ml milk
1 medium onion, chopped
8oz/225g mushrooms, chopped
1–2oz/25–55g butter or margarine
1 tablespoon soy sauce
1 × 4½oz/128g packet TVP mince or 4 vegetable burgers, crumbled
12fl.oz/340ml tomato juice (6fl.oz/170ml if using vegetable burgers)
2 eggs, beaten
8oz/225g mashed potatoes
salt and freshly ground black pepper to taste
2 tablespoons chopped fresh herbs, to taste

Pre-heat the oven to 350°F/180°C (Gas Mark 4). Lightly grease a 2lb/910g loaf tin and line it with greaseproof paper. Soak the breadcrumbs in the milk and put on one side for 10 minutes.

Sauté the onion and mushrooms in the butter until light brown, then add the soy sauce and the TVP mince. Pour in the tomato juice and simmer for 4–5 minutes. In a separate bowl, mix all the other ingredients.

Add the soaked breadcrumbs and the sauté to the mixture in the bowl. Mix very well and press into the loaf tin.

Bake for 1 hour. Leave in the tin for 5 minutes before turning out on to a serving dish.

1 hour 30 minutes to make
Good source of protein, vitamin A, B group vitamins, vitamin C

Mushroom Pie

12oz/340g shortcrust pastry (enough for an 8 inch/20cm two-crust pie)
2oz/55g butter or margarine
1 medium onion, chopped
2 tablespoons plain flour
7–10fl.oz/205–290ml cream or milk
1 tablespoon brandy or sherry
1 tablespoon chopped fresh tarragon
salt and freshly ground black pepper to taste
1lb/455g mushrooms, chopped

Pre-heat the oven to 400°F/200°C (Gas Mark 6). Line a greased pie dish with half of the pastry, so that it overhangs the edges by approximately ½ inch/ 1.2cm.

Melt the butter in a saucepan and sauté the onion until tender. Sprinkle the flour over the onion and stir well as it thickens. Keep the pan over a low heat and gradually add the cream, stirring constantly to create a thick, smooth sauce.

Add the brandy, tarragon, salt and pepper and mix well, still over a low heat. Stir the mushrooms into the sauce and cook for 2 minutes, then remove from the heat and pour this mixture into the prepared pie dish.

Roll out the other half of the pastry, cut into strips and weave together to make a pretty lattice top for the pie. (Alternatively, you can just roll the crust in the ordinary manner and place it over the pie filling, decorating it with long cuts to let the steam out.) Crimp and trim the edges of the pastry and bake for 25–30 minutes, until the crust is golden brown.

50 minutes to make
Good source of protein, B group vitamins, potassium

Olive and Steaklet Bake

To prevent curdling, make sure you don't put the casserole back in the oven after adding the sour cream. Covering the casserole at the last stage of the recipe will ensure that the cream is warmed through.

2 tablespoons vegetable oil
6 vegetable burgers
4 cloves garlic, crushed or 2 teaspoons garlic powder
1 × 12oz/340g bottle pimento-stuffed olives, chopped
1 teaspoon mild mustard
1 tablespoon chopped spring onion
1 tablespoon pickle
15fl.oz/430ml vegetable stock or water
8fl.oz/230ml sour cream

Pre-heat the oven to 350°F/180°C (Gas Mark 4) and lightly grease a casserole dish. Heat the oil in a frying pan over a medium heat. Put in the burgers and brown them on both sides, about 5 minutes in total, then place them on a plate.

Press the garlic on to both sides of the burgers, and place them in the casserole dish.

Add the olives and the rest of the ingredients, apart from the sour cream, to the frying pan. Stir over a medium heat for 3–5 minutes.

Pour this sauce over the burgers and bake, uncovered, for 45 minutes. Remove from the oven. Pour the sour cream over the burgers. Cover the casserole and leave for 5 minutes. Serve immediately.

1 hour 10 minutes to make
Good source of vitamin A

Penne with Vodka

A friend and fellow pasta-lover passed this on to me – serve with a green salad.

1 tablespoon olive oil
1 small onion, finely chopped
2–3 chillies, finely chopped
1 teaspoon dried basil or 2 fresh leaves
4 tablespoons vodka
1×14oz/397g tin tomatoes
1 tablespoon tomato puree
1lb/455g pasta (Penne)
8fl.oz/230ml single cream
4oz/115g Parmesan cheese
freshly ground black pepper to taste

Heat the oil in a saucepan and lightly sauté the onions, then add the chillies and fry for 2–3 minutes.

Add the basil and half the vodka to the saucepan, then increase the heat and add the tomatoes and tomato puree, breaking up the tomatoes with a wooden spoon. Bring to the boil, then reduce the heat and simmer, uncovered, for about 30 minutes, until you have a thick sauce.

Cook the pasta until it's tender (al dente). While it's cooking, add the remaining 2 tablespoons of vodka to the sauce.

When the pasta has cooked, drain it and turn it into the sauce. Take the saucepan off the heat and slowly add the cream, tossing it all together in the pan. Add the Parmesan and black pepper, and serve immediately.

50 minutes to make
Good source of protein, vitamin A, vitamin C, calcium

Pepper Steaklets

   6 vegetable burgers
   2 tablespoons olive oil
   3 tablespoons whole peppercorns, crushed
   ½oz/15g butter or margarine
   8 tablespoons red wine
   2 tablespoons brandy
   salt and freshly ground black pepper to taste
   1 clove garlic, crushed

Brush the burgers with a little oil, and pat the peppercorns on to both sides.

Heat the remaining oil in a frying pan and brown the burgers on both sides (about 5 minutes in total). Reduce the heat and cook, covered, for 8 minutes.

Remove the burgers from the pan and keep them warm. Add the butter, wine, brandy, salt, pepper and garlic to the pan. Heat it well, stirring until it starts to bubble, then reduce the heat for 3–4 minutes.

Pour the hot sauce over the burgers and serve immediately with vegetables.

20 minutes to make

Peruvian Burgers

Serve with rice or potatoes and a green vegetable such as broccoli.

1oz/25g butter or margarine
6 vegetable burgers, cubed
2 medium onions, chopped
2 teaspoons ground cumin
1 × 14oz/397g tin chopped tomatoes
2 tablespoons tomato ketchup
2fl.oz/60ml white wine
salt and freshly ground black pepper to taste
12 stuffed olives
1½oz/45g flaked almonds
2oz/55g raisins

Melt the butter in a frying pan and brown the burger chunks (about 5 minutes in total). Remove them from the pan and place on one side.

Sauté the onions in the butter until lightly browned. Add the cumin and cook for 1 minute to draw out the flavour.

Add the remaining ingredients to the sauté and stir well. Bring the mixture to a gentle boil, then add the burger chunks. Cover the pan, reduce the heat and simmer for 30 minutes.

45 minutes to make
Good source of vitamin A, vitamin C

Potato Torte à la Faranto

This is based on a fabulous Spanish/Mexican dish (torte means 'cake') which must be served piping hot.

for the sauce:
3 tablespoons olive oil
1 small onion, chopped
½ stick celery, chopped
2 cloves garlic, crushed
1 × 14oz/397g tin chopped tomatoes
1 tablespoon tomato puree
1 bay leaf
½ teaspoon dried basil
½ teaspoon dried oregano
1 teaspoon chopped fresh parsley

for the potatoes:
1¼lb/570g potatoes, peeled and cubed
½oz/15g butter or margarine
2 tablespoons milk
1 egg, beaten
¼ teaspoon salt
2oz/55g plain flour
1 tablespoon olive oil
4oz/115g Mozzarella cheese, grated
3 tablespoons grated Parmesan cheese

Pre-heat the oven to 350°F/180°C (Gas Mark 4) and grease an ovenproof dish. Make the sauce first – the longer ahead you make it, the better it tastes. Heat the oil in a saucepan and sauté the onions, celery, and garlic together until lightly browned. Then add the tomatoes, the tomato puree and the bay leaf, and simmer over a very low heat for 45 minutes. Add the basil, oregano and parsley for the last 10 minutes of simmering time.

Boil the potatoes until soft (about 25 minutes). Put them in a mixing bowl and mash them together with the butter, milk and egg. Add the salt and flour and work the mash together very well.

Press the potato mixture into the bottom and sides of the gratin dish to a thickness of ½ inch/1.2cm. Sprinkle with the olive oil and bake this potato shell for 15 minutes.

Pour the sauce into the baked potato shell to a depth of ¾ inch/2cm and sprinkle the Mozzarella and Parmesan over the sauce. Bake for

10–20 minutes, until the cheeses are bubbly and the edges of the potato are lightly browned.

1 hour 30 minutes to make
Good source of protein, vitamin A, vitamin C, calcium

Rice and Beans

6oz/170g dried navy beans or similar beans
1oz/25g butter or margarine
1 medium onion, chopped
1 stick celery, chopped
1 × 14oz/397g tin chopped tomatoes
12fl.oz/340ml water
8oz/225g long grain rice
salt and freshly ground black pepper to taste

Wash then soak the beans overnight. Bring to the boil in plenty of fresh water and boil rapidly for 10 minutes. Simmer for 40–45 minutes or until soft.

Melt the butter in a saucepan and lightly brown the onions and celery.

Add the beans, tomatoes, water and rice. Stir well, cover and cook for about 20 minutes until all the water has been absorbed. Season to taste and serve immediately.

1 hour 20 minutes to make
Good source of vitamin A, B group vitamins, vitamin C

Rice and Vegetables in Wine

2 tablespoons vegetable oil
1 onion, chopped
1 medium courgette, chopped
1 medium carrot, chopped
1 stick celery, chopped
8oz/225g long grain rice
12fl.oz/340ml vegetable stock or water
8fl.oz/230ml white wine

Heat the oil in a saucepan and sauté the onion. Add the rest of the vegetables and stir them over a medium heat until lightly browned.

Add the rice, vegetable stock and white wine, cover and cook for about 15–20 minutes until all the liquid has been absorbed.

30 minutes to make
Good source of vitamin A

Rice in Tasty Vegetable Stock

4 tablespoons vegetable oil
1 large onion, chopped
1½lb/680g mushrooms, chopped
1 clove garlic, crushed
8oz/225g long grain rice
2 tablespoons wild rice (optional)
1 pint/570ml vegetable stock or water
2 tablespoons dried mixed herbs
salt and freshly ground black pepper to taste

Heat the oil in a large saucepan and sauté the onion, mushrooms and garlic over a low flame.

Add the rice and stir for 1–2 minutes to soak up the flavour.

Cover the rice with the vegetable stock and add the herbs and seasoning. Put a lid on the pan and gently simmer for about 20 minutes, until the liquid has been absorbed and the rice is tender and fluffy.

35 minutes to make
Good source of vitamin A, B group vitamins, vitamin C, potassium

Rice with Asparagus

1½lb/680g asparagus spears
3oz/85g butter or margarine
8oz/225g long grain rice (part wild rice, if desired)
1 pint/570ml vegetable stock or water
salt and freshly ground black pepper to taste
3oz/85g Parmesan cheese, grated

Trim any woody stems from the asparagus. Melt the butter in a saucepan, add the asparagus tips and sauté for 2–3 minutes.

Add the rice, vegetable stock and seasoning, cover and simmer on a low heat for 15–20 minutes, until the rice is dry and fluffy.

Sprinkle with cheese and serve hot.

30 minutes to make
Good source of protein, vitamin A, B group vitamins, vitamin C

Sauté Schnitzel

1oz/25g butter or margarine
6 vegetable schnitzels or vegetable burgers
8 tablespoons white wine
1 teaspoon lemon juice
1 clove garlic, crushed

for the garnish:
1 tablespoon chopped fresh parsley

Melt the butter in a frying pan and brown the burgers on both sides (about 5 minutes in total), then remove them from the pan.

Add the white wine, lemon juice and garlic to the saucepan and cook for 1 minute. Bring to a slow boil and let the wine reduce slightly.

Place the burgers back in the pan and heat them thoroughly for another 3 minutes. Serve immediately, over rice or toast, with a garnish of fresh parsley.

10 minutes to make

Savoury Rice

Serve with steamed vegetables or salad.

1 tablespoon vegetable oil
1 medium onion, chopped
8oz/225g long grain rice (part wild rice if desired)
1 pint/570ml vegetable stock or water
1 tablespoon soy sauce

Heat the oil in a deep saucepan and sauté the onion.

Add the rice to the sauté and stir over a medium heat until the rice begins to go clear.

Add the vegetable stock and soy sauce and cook, covered, for about 15–20 minutes, or until the liquid has been absorbed. Stir and serve hot.

30 minutes to make
Good source of vitamin A

Savoury Turnovers

Serve hot with a selection of vegetables.

½oz/15g butter or margarine
1 medium onion, chopped
1 clove garlic, crushed (optional)
4 vegetable burgers, crumbled
2 tablespoons chopped fresh parsley
2 tablespoons chopped fresh chives
4fl.oz/120ml sour cream
1 teaspoon cornflour
salt and freshly ground black pepper to taste
12oz/340g shortcrust pastry

Pre-heat the oven to 400°F/200°C (Gas Mark 6) and lightly grease a baking tray. Melt the butter in a large frying pan and sauté the onion and garlic until lightly browned.

Crumble the burgers into the sauté with the parsley and chives. Stir for 5 minutes, until the burgers begin to brown.

Mix the sour cream with the cornflour and add enough to the burger mixture to make it moist but not sloppy. Stir to an even consistency and season to taste. Roll the pastry and cut into 5 inch/12.5cm rounds.

Place a spoonful of the filling on each pastry round and fold the pastry over. Crimp the edges, prick the top with a fork and arrange on the baking tray. Bake for 15 minutes. Serve hot or cold.

Schnitzel Scaloppini in White Wine

Serve over noodles or rice with green vegetables.

1½oz/45g butter or margarine
6 vegetable burgers, sliced in half
6fl.oz/180ml vegetable stock
1 clove garlic, crushed
4 tablespoons white wine

Melt the butter in a large frying pan and brown the burgers (about 5 minutes in total). Remove them from the pan and place in a hot oven to keep warm.

Add the stock, garlic and wine to the hot oil and bring to the boil. Pour the hot sauce over the hot burgers, and serve immediately.

15 minutes to make
Good source of protein

Shepherd's Pie

If you like a slightly stronger flavour, try adding 2 large carrots, thinly sliced, to the onion as it sautés.

1½lb/680g potatoes
3oz/85g butter or margarine
1–2 tablespoons milk
1 large onion, chopped
1 × 4½oz/128g packet TVP mince or 6 vegetable burgers, crumbled
2 tablespoons soy sauce
15fl.oz/430ml vegetable stock or water (7fl.oz if using vegetable burgers)
salt and freshly ground black pepper to taste

Pre-heat the oven to 400°F/200°C (Gas Mark 6). Boil the potatoes and mash them in a bowl with 2oz/55g of the butter and enough milk to give a good sticky consistency. Put them to one side.

Melt the remaining butter in a frying pan and sauté the onion. Then add the TVP mince, soy sauce and vegetable stock. Simmer for 5–10 minutes. Season to taste.

If you want a thicker mixture, blend a little flour or vegetable gravy mix with some vegetable stock and add to the sauté. Cook until thickened, stirring constantly. Pour the mixture into a baking dish and cover with the mashed potatoes.

Bake for 30 minutes, until the potatoes are nice and brown. For extra browning on top, just place under the grill for a few moments (make sure your baking dish will stand this treatment).

1 hour 15 minutes to make
Good source of vitamin A, B group vitamins, vitamin C, potassium

Simple Beefless Hash

12oz/340g potatoes
1oz/25g butter or margarine
1 large onion, chopped
2 teaspoons mixed herbs
1 tablespoon vegetable extract
1 × 4½oz/128g packet TVP chunks
12fl.oz/340ml vegetable stock or water
2 tablespoons tomato puree
salt and freshly ground black pepper to taste

Peel and dice the potatoes, and parboil them for 1 minute, then drain. Melt the butter in a frying pan and sauté the onion and garlic. Then add the herbs.

Add the diced potato and sauté for 2–3 minutes. Now add the vegetable extract and TVP chunks and stir for 2–3 minutes over a low heat.

Stir in the vegetable stock, tomato puree and seasoning. Cover and simmer over a low heat for 15 minutes, adding a little extra stock or water if necessary to make a thick sauce.

25 minutes to make
Good source of vitamin A, vitamin C

Sour Cream Soufflé

4oz/115g plain flour
salt and freshly ground black pepper to taste
2oz/55g Gruyère cheese, grated
12fl.oz/340ml sour cream
5 eggs, separated

Pre-heat the oven to 350°F/180°C (Gas Mark 4) and grease a 2–2½ pints/ 1.1–1.4l soufflé dish. Mix the flour, salt, pepper and grated cheese together in a mixing bowl. Then stir in the sour cream.

Whisk the egg yolks in a small bowl and add them to the sour cream mixture. Stir well.

In a large mixing bowl, beat the egg whites until they are very stiff. Then fold them gently into the sour cream mixture.

Pour the mixture into the soufflé dish and set this dish in a pan filled with water. Place together in the oven and bake for 40 minutes.

1 hour to make
Good source of vitamin A, B group vitamins, calcium

Sour Cream, Paprika and Mushrooms

Serve hot over rice, mashed potatoes or toast with broccoli, spinach or any green vegetable.

1oz/25g butter or margarine
1 medium onion, chopped
1 clove garlic, crushed
1lb/455g mushrooms, sliced
1 teaspoon paprika
8fl.oz/230ml sour cream
salt and freshly ground black pepper to taste

Melt the butter in a frying pan and sauté the onion and garlic until tender. Add the mushrooms and cook gently for a further 3 minutes. Drain off most of the juice, but do not discard.

Add the paprika and cook briefly.

Remove the mixture from the heat and stir in the sour cream. You may return it to the heat, but do not let it boil. Add a little of the drained mushroom juice if the mushrooms need more sauce. Season to taste.

15 minutes to make
Good source of B group vitamins

Spaghetti Omelette

Serves 2.

2oz/55g uncooked spaghetti or 4oz/115g left-over cooked spaghetti
2 eggs
1oz/25g butter or margarine
salt and freshly ground black pepper to taste
2oz/55g Cheddar cheese, grated

If using raw spaghetti, bring a pan of water to a galloping boil and break the spaghetti into it. Leave the pan uncovered and boil the spaghetti for 10–12 minutes. Drain.

Whisk the eggs in a mixing bowl and add the cooked spaghetti.

Heat the butter in a frying pan and pour in the egg and spaghetti mixture. Season, and leave the omelette to cook for 1 minute. Sprinkle the grated cheese over the omelette, then leave to cook for a further 1–2 minutes. Use a spatula to fold the omelette over. Serve piping hot with toast or a salad.

15 minutes to make
Good source of protein, vitamin A, B group vitamins, calcium, zinc

Spanish Burgers

Serve hot with rice or mashed potatoes.

2oz/55g butter or margarine
8 vegetable burgers, cubed
1 medium onion, chopped
2 sticks celery, chopped
3 carrots, chopped
1 green pepper, deseeded and chopped
8oz/225g mushrooms, chopped
1 × 14oz/397g tin chopped tomatoes
1 bay leaf
2 teaspoons paprika
salt and freshly ground black pepper to taste
6oz/170g petits pois
juice of ½ lemon

Melt half of the butter in a large saucepan and brown the burger chunks, about 5 minutes in total. Remove them from the pan and place to one side. Melt the rest of the butter and sauté the onion and celery.

When the onion and celery are tender, return the burger chunks to the pan and stir gently.

Add all the remaining ingredients except the petits pois and lemon juice. Stir well and cover the pan. Simmer gently for 30 minutes.

Add the peas and simmer for a further 5 minutes, stirring often. Pour in the lemon juice. Serve immediately.

50 minutes to make
Good source of vitamin A, B group vitamins, vitamin C

Spanish Omelette

1oz/25g butter or margarine
1 medium onion, chopped
3 sticks celery, chopped
½ red or green pepper, deseeded and chopped (optional)
2 tomatoes, chopped
2 tablespoons tomato puree
4 eggs, beaten

Melt half the butter in a frying pan and sauté the onion until it is soft.

Add the celery and pepper. Stir well until the onion begins to brown, then add the tomatoes. Cook over a low heat and stir for about 8–10 minutes, adding little more butter if necessary. Stir in the tomato puree.

Put the rest of the butter in a frying pan over a medium heat and add the eggs. Leave the eggs untouched until they begin to cook through, then use a spatula to lift the omelette and turn it over. Place the vegetables on the cooked side, and when the other side is cooked, fold in half and serve immediately.

20 minutes to make
Good source of protein, vitamin A, B group vitamins, vitamin C, iron

Spicy Eggs

3 tablespoons olive oil
1 large onion, chopped
1 clove garlic, crushed
1 green pepper, deseeded and sliced
4 large mushrooms, chopped
1 teaspoon chilli powder (or more to taste)
½ teaspoon cumin seed
½ teaspoon oregano
salt and freshly ground black pepper to taste
6 eggs
6oz/170g Cheddar cheese, grated

Pre-heat the oven to 350°F/180°C (Gas Mark 4) and lightly oil a baking dish. Heat the oil in a large pan and sauté the onion and garlic for 3–4 minutes, then add the green pepper and mushrooms and cook for approximately 5 minutes.

Add the spices, herb and seasonings. Stir often as the mixture cooks for a further 5 minutes.

Pour the mixture into the baking dish and break the eggs over it. Cover with the grated cheese and bake for 15–20 minutes. Serve hot.

40 minutes to make
Good source of protein, vitamin A, vitamin C, calcium

Spinach and Sour Cream Omelette

Serve with steamed carrots and peas or a fresh salad. Serves 2.

8oz/225g fresh spinach
½ clove garlic, crushed
pinch of nutmeg
salt and freshly ground black pepper to taste
2fl.oz/60ml sour cream
½ oz/15g butter or margarine
1 large egg
1 tablespoon milk
fresh herbs to taste

Wash and trim the spinach, removing all the stems, and place in a very hot frying pan. Cover, and simmer the spinach in its own juice until it is tender. Then drain off all the liquid and reduce the heat.

Chop the drained spinach while it is still in the pan (use a spatula), then add the garlic, nutmeg, salt, pepper and sour cream. Stir together over a low heat, but don't allow this mixture to boil.

Melt the butter in a frying pan. Beat the egg and milk together in a jug and pour into the hot butter. Cook for 1 minute over a high heat. Use a spatula to lift the omelette and turn it over.

Spoon the spinach mixture on to the centre of the omelette as it finishes cooking. Spread the filling round to the edges of half the omelette, sprinkle with fresh herbs, then use the spatula to fold the omelette over. Lift the omelette out of the pan and slice it in half.

20 minutes to make
Good source of protein, vitamin A, B group vitamins, vitamin C, iron

Spinach Cheese Dumplings

A wonderful, tasty winter warmer – serve with a selection of vegatables.

1lb/ 455g fresh spinach
8oz/225g cottage or ricotta cheese
2 egg yolks, beaten
4oz/115g Parmesan cheese, grated
salt and freshly ground black pepper to taste
pinch of nutmeg
2oz/55g self-raising flour
2oz/55g butter or margarine

Wash and trim the spinach and cook it, covered, in its own juices. Drain very well, chop finely and allow to cool.

Mix the cottage cheese, egg yolks, half the Parmesan cheese, the salt, pepper and nutmeg in a large mixing bowl. Add the cooled spinach and the flour and mix together.

Take a spoonful of the mixture and using a little flour shape it into a small ball, flouring your hands if necessary. Continue in this way until all the mixture is used.

Drop the dumplings into a pot of boiling water, about 10–12 at a time, and cook for 4–5 minutes. Continue in this way until all the dumplings are cooked.

Melt the butter. Place the dumplings on a hot serving dish and pour the butter over them. Sprinkle with the remaining Parmesan cheese and serve immediately.

35 minutes to make
Good source of protein, vitamin A, vitamin C, calcium, iron

Spinach Pie

6oz/170g shortcrust pastry
1lb/455g fresh spinach, finely chopped
4 eggs
8fl.oz/230ml sour cream
½oz/15g butter or margarine
1oz/25g Cheddar cheese, grated
2oz/55g fresh breadcrumbs

Pre-heat the oven to 425°F/220°C (Gas Mark 7) and grease a 12 inch/30cm flan dish. Roll out the pastry to fit the dish, press it in and bake blind for 7 minutes. Remove from the oven and reduce the oven temperature to 350°F/180°C (Gas Mark 4).

Press the spinach into the pastry case.

Beat the eggs and sour cream together and pour them over the spinach.

Melt the butter and mix it with the cheese and breadcrumbs. Spread this mixture over the sour cream. Bake the pie for 30 minutes, until the top is golden. Serve hot.

45 minutes to make
Good source of vitamin A, B group vitamins, vitamin C, calcium

Steaklets Diane

Serve on a warmed plate with new potatoes, green beans and sautéd mushrooms.

2oz/55g butter or margarine
4 vegetable burgers
1 tablespoon warmed brandy
1 tablespoon sherry
1 tablespoon finely chopped chives or onion

Pre-heat the oven to 350°F/180°C (Gas Mark 4). Melt 1½oz/40g of the butter in a frying pan and brown the burgers on both sides (about 5 minutes in total). Remove the burgers from the pan and put them in the hot oven.

Add the brandy, sherry and the rest of the butter to the frying pan. Sprinkle the chives over it and stir well.

Return the burgers to the frying pan and cook them in the sauce for 1 minute. Serve immediately.

15 minutes to make
Good source of protein

Steaklets Pepper

Serve with wild rice, mashed potatoes or macaroni with any green vegetable and glazed carrots.

  3 tablespoons vegetable oil
  4 vegetable burgers
  1 large onion, chopped
  1 clove garlic, crushed
  2 green peppers, deseeded and chopped
  8fl.oz/230ml vegetable stock or water
  1 × 14oz/397g tin chopped tomatoes
  1½ tablespoons cornstarch
  1 tablespoon soy sauce

Pre-heat the oven to 350°F/180°C (Gas Mark 4). Heat the oil in a large saucepan and brown the burgers on both sides (about 5 minutes in total). Remove the burgers from the pan and place in a hot oven. Add the onions and garlic to the pan and sauté until they are tender.

Add the peppers and most of the vegetable stock to the sauté, then cover and simmer for 10 minutes.

Add the tomatoes and simmer for a further 10 minutes. Mix the cornflour and soy sauce with the remaining vegetable stock to make a smooth, lump-free paste. Add this to the sauce and continue to simmer.

When the sauce has thickened, return the burgers to the pan. Increase the heat for 1 minute. Serve immediately.

30 minutes to make
Good source of protein, vitamin C

Stuffed Eggs and Tomato

Serve with steamed vegetables.

6 eggs
1½oz/45g butter or margarine
4 tablespoons tomato puree
1 teaspoon mild mustard
salt and freshly ground black pepper to taste
15fl.oz/430ml béchamel sauce (see page 143)

for the garnish:
1 tablespoon chopped fresh parsley

Pre-heat the oven to 350°F/180°C (Gas Mark 4) and lightly grease a baking dish.

Hard-boil the eggs – about 10 minutes in boiling water. Peel the eggs and slice them in half lengthways. Remove the yolks and place them in a mixing bowl.

Blend the yolks, butter, half the tomato puree and the mustard to make a smooth paste. Fill the egg whites with this mixture and place them in the baking dish.

Combine the remaining tomato puree, salt, pepper and béchamel sauce and pour it over the stuffed eggs.

Bake for 15–20 minutes. Sprinkle the parsley over the hot sauce and serve immediately.

40 minutes to make
Good source of protein, vitamin A

Stuffed Peppers

4oz/115g long grain rice (can be part wild)
4 medium red or green or yellow peppers, halved vertically and deseeded
4 tablespoons vegetable oil
1 large onion, chopped
half a 4½oz/128g packet TVP mince
2 tablespoons chopped fresh parsley
1 pint/20fl.oz Fresh Tomato Sauce (see page 145)
salt and freshly ground black pepper to taste

Pre-heat the oven to 375°F/190°C (Gas Mark 5). Cover the rice with twice its volume of water in a medium-sized saucepan. Bring to the boil, then cover the pan, reduce the heat and leave the rice to simmer for about 20 minutes, or until all the water is absorbed.

Arrange the pepper halves in a large baking dish. Heat the oil in a saucepan and sauté the onion until it is soft. Add the TVP mince and stir well. Add the parsley and cook over a low heat for 5 minutes.

Add the cooked rice and half the tomato sauce. Mix well, season to taste, and spoon the mixture into the pepper halves.

Pour some of the remaining tomato sauce over each stuffed pepper. Cover and bake for 30 minutes. Serve immediately.

1 hour to make
Good source of vitamin A, vitamin C

Sunday Breakfast

This makes a lovely, traditional plate for Sunday breakfast – we all look forward to it!

for the tomato sauce:
½oz/15g butter or margarine
2 × 14oz/397g tins chopped tomatoes
salt and freshly ground black pepper to taste
for the bangers:
5oz/140g vegetable sausage mix
½ teaspoon each chopped fresh thyme and chopped rosemary, or 1½ teaspoons dried mixed herbs
2 teaspoons chopped fresh parsley
½ teaspoon chopped fresh sage
1 teaspoon garlic powder
1 egg, beaten
1 teaspoon freshly ground black pepper
½oz/15g butter or margarine

to serve:
fried eggs
toast

Set the sauce to simmer gently first of all, since it will take the longest to cook. Melt the butter in a saucepan and empty the chopped tomatoes, salt and pepper into it. Simmer, stirring often, until enough water has evaporated for it to take on a thickish consistency.

Make up the vegetable sausage mix according to the directions on the packet, adding the herbs, garlic powder, beaten egg and seasonings. Mix well. Let the mixture stand for 5–10 minutes, until firm enough to mould into sausage shapes. Melt the butter in the frying pan and brown the sausages, turning often.

Keep the sausages warm while you prepare fried eggs and toast for the family. Serve everything together on warm plates.

25 minutes to make
Good source of vitamin A, vitamin C

Super Curried Eggs Indian Style

Serve with rice.

6 eggs
2oz/55g butter or margarine
1 medium onion, chopped
1 clove garlic, crushed
2 tablespoons curry powder
2 tablespoons tomato puree
6fl.oz/180ml water
1 tablespoon lemon juice
salt and freshly ground black pepper to taste
rind of 1 lemon, grated
2 tablespoons fresh parsley, chopped

Hard-boil the eggs for 10 minutes.

Melt the butter in a frying pan and sauté the onion and garlic. Add the curry powder, tomato puree, water, lemon juice, salt and pepper. Stir all these ingredients together. Allow the mixture to cook over a low heat until it is just bubbling.

When the eggs have finished cooking, peel them and slice them in half lengthways. Add these to the curry and stir gently.

Add the lemon rind and the parsley to the curry. Stir once again, and serve hot.

30 minutes to make
Good source of protein, vitamin A, B group vitamins, vitamin C, iron

Swiss Fondue

Perhaps a bit exotic, but it's a great recipe, and will give you something to do with that fondue set you got as a present! Fun for a party.

15fl.oz/430ml white wine
1 clove garlic, crushed
1lb/455g Gruyère or other Swiss cheese, grated
½oz/15g plain flour
salt and freshly ground black pepper to taste

to serve:
French bread

Using a fireproof dish, heat the wine over a low heat until it begins to bubble gently. Add the garlic.

Mix the cheese, flour, salt and pepper together in a bowl.

Gradually add this mixture to the hot wine, stirring constantly to make a very smooth sauce. Keep the sauce hot over a low heat, stirring from time to time to stop it getting too thick and solid.

Cut the French bread into cubes and give each person a long-handled fork with which to dip the bread cubes into the fondue. Eat immediately!

25 minutes to make
Good source of protein, vitamin A, calcium

Swiss Schnitzel

Serve with salad, hot vegetables or baked potatoes.

4 tablespoons olive oil
6 vegetable schnitzels or vegetable burgers
salt and freshly ground black pepper to taste
4 tablespoons lemon juice
4 eggs
2 tablespoons chopped fresh parsley

Pre-heat the oven to 350°F/180°C (Gas Mark 4). Heat 1 tablespoon of the oil in a frying pan and brown the schnitzels (about 5 minutes in total). Place them on an ovenproof plate. Sprinkle the schnitzels with salt, pepper and lemon juice, and put them in the hot oven to keep warm.

Heat the remaining oil and fry the eggs.

Remove the schnitzels from the oven, sprinkle some parsley over each, then top each pair with a fried egg. Pour some of the hot lemon juice over each egg and serve immediately.

20 minutes to make
Good source of protein, B group vitamins, vitamin C

Swiss Steaklets

Serve with rice or green vegetables.

4oz/115g butter or margarine
1 large onion, chopped
1 clove garlic, crushed
4oz/115g fresh mushrooms, sliced (optional)
6 vegetable burgers
1 × 14oz/397g tin chopped tomatoes
1 × 5oz/140g tin tomato puree
12fl.oz/340ml tomato juice or water

Pre-heat the oven to 350°F/180°C (Gas Mark 4). Melt the butter in a large frying pan and sauté the onion, garlic and mushrooms until golden brown. Then add as many burgers as will fit into the pan and brown them on both sides (about 5 minutes in total).

Take the burgers out and place them in the warm oven. Add the tomatoes, tomato puree and juice to the pan. Bring to the boil and keep them boiling for 3 minutes, stirring.

Finally turn the heat down to a simmer, put the burgers back into the sauce, cover and cook for 10 minutes. Serve hot.

30 minutes to make
Good source of protein, vitamin A, vitamin C

Teriyaki

Serve the marinated burger chunks over rice or with other vegetables, with a spoonful of the hot sauce to accompany them.

6 vegetable burgers, cubed
1 medium onion, chopped
1 clove garlic, crushed
1 tablespoon fresh grated ginger or 1 teaspoon ground ginger
8 tablespoons soy sauce
8 tablespoons vegetable oil
8 tablespoons orange juice
1 tablespoon lemon juice
3 teaspoons sugar

Place the burger chunks in a deep dish. Mix all the other ingredients together in a large jug or bowl and pour over the burger chunks. Cover, and leave to marinate for 4–6 hours.

At the end of that time, drain the sauce into a saucepan and bring to a simmer. Grill or barbecue the burger chunks until nicely browned.

6 hours 30 minutes to make
Good source of protein

Tomato Pie

8oz/225g shortcrust pastry
2 tablespoons olive oil
2 onions, chopped
1 clove garlic, crushed
1 small courgette, chopped
6 large tomatoes, peeled or 1 × 14oz/397g tin chopped tomatoes
4 tablespoons chopped fresh parsley
1 teaspoon dried sage
1 teaspoon chopped tarragon
salt and freshly ground black pepper to taste
2 eggs, beaten
4oz/115g Cheddar cheese, grated

Preheat the oven to 425°F/220°C (Gas Mark 7). Line an 8 inch/20cm flan dish with the shortcrust pastry and bake blind for 3–4 minutes. Reduce the heat to 400°F/200°C (Gas Mark 6).

Heat the oil in a saucepan and sauté the onions, garlic and courgette until lightly browned.

Add the tomatoes, herbs and seasoning and simmer this mixture for a further 5 minutes. Pour the sauté into the pie crust.

Pour the beaten eggs over the sauté mixture, top with the grated cheese and bake for 15 minutes. Serve hot.

30 minutes to make
Good source of protein, vitamin A, B group vitamins, vitamin C, calcium

Tomato Rice

For a tasty variation, try adding 1–2 teaspoons of oregano to the tomatoes, or add 4oz/115g grated cheese at the end of cooking and stir until melted.

2oz/55g butter or margarine
1 large onion, chopped
8oz/225g long grain rice
2 × 14oz/397g tins chopped tomatoes
2 tablespoons tomato puree
15fl.oz/430ml tomato juice
a little extra boiling vegetable stock or water

Melt the butter in a large saucepan and sauté the onion until tender.

Add the rice and stir well. Add the tomatoes, tomato puree and tomato juice and bring the mixture to a boil. Cover, reduce the heat and simmer for 25–35 minutes or until the rice is tender. Check on the liquid content towards the end of cooking, and add boiling stock if necessary. Serve hot.

45 minutes to make
Good source of vitamin A, vitamin C, potassium

Tomato Soufflé

A wonderful soufflé, easy to make and tasty to eat. Serve with fresh green vegetables or a salad.

6 large tomatoes, peeled
1oz/25g butter or margarine
3 tablespoons tomato puree
1 tablespoon sugar
1 tablespoon chopped fresh parsley
salt and freshly ground black pepper to taste
8fl.oz/230ml thick White Sauce (see page 150)
3 tablespoons grated Swiss or Parmesan cheese
5 eggs, separated

for the garnish:
sprig of fresh basil

Pre-heat the oven to 400°F/200°C (Gas Mark 6) and grease an 8 inch/ 20cm soufflé dish. Chop the tomatoes and put them in a frying pan with the butter. Cook over a medium heat for 5–6 minutes, until the liquid reduces.

Add the tomato puree, sugar, parsley, salt and pepper to the frying pan and stir well. Add the white sauce and cheese, stir thoroughly and remove from the heat. Leave to cool slightly.

Beat the egg yolks in a small bowl, then stir them into the tomato mixture. In a separate, larger bowl, beat the egg whites until they are very stiff. Gently fold the beaten egg whites into the tomato mixture and pour the whole mixture into the soufflé dish.

Bake for 35–40 minutes, until well risen and golden. Garnish with the fresh basil and serve immediately.

55 minutes to make
Good source of protein, vitamin A, B group vitamins, vitamin C, iron

CASSEROLES AND STEWS

Asparagus and Egg Casserole

This is a luxurious casserole dish which is best accompanied by a light salad or vegetable dish such as New Orleans Broad Beans (see page 113).

4 eggs
1½lb/680g asparagus spears
2oz/55g butter or margarine
1oz/25g plain flour
14fl.oz/400ml vegetable stock or water
2fl.oz/ 60ml cream
¼ teaspoon ground nutmeg (optional)
1 teaspoon chopped tarragon
salt and freshly ground black pepper to taste
2oz/55g Cheddar cheese, grated

Pre-heat the oven to 400°F/200°C (Gas Mark 6) and lightly grease a casserole dish. Place the eggs in boiling water for 10 minutes, until they are hard-boiled.

Wash and trim the asparagus. Simmer or steam it, in batches if necessary, for 4–5 minutes, depending on the thickness of the spears. Drain the asparagus when cooked.

Melt the butter in a saucepan and sprinkle the flour into it, stirring constantly to make a thick paste. In another saucepan, mix the vegetable stock and cream together and heat to a low boil.

Gradually add the stock and cream mixture to the flour paste, stirring constantly to make a creamy sauce. Add the nutmeg, tarragon, salt and pepper and continue to stir. Peel and chop the hard-boiled eggs and add them to the sauce. Stir gently and remove from the heat.

Arrange the asparagus spears in the bottom of the casserole dish and pour the sauce over them. Sprinkle the grated cheese over the sauce and bake for 15 minutes until the cheese is bubbly.

50 minutes to make
Good source of vitamin A, B group vitamins, vitamin C

Asparagus Casserole with Sour Cream

When you feel like a change, try adding the juice of one lemon to the sour cream before pouring it over the asparagus. Serve with a salad or any vegetable.

1½lb/680g asparagus spears
salt and freshly ground black pepper to taste
1 clove garlic, crushed
2 teaspoons cornflour
10fl.oz/290ml sour cream
1oz/25g fresh breadcrumbs
2 teaspoons chopped fresh tarragon (optional)
1oz/25g butter or margarine

Pre-heat the oven to 375°F/190°C (Gas Mark 5) and lightly grease a casserole dish. Wash, trim and simmer or steam the asparagus spears, in batches if necessary, for 4–5 minutes depending on the thickness of the spears. Drain well and arrange in the casserole dish.

Sprinkle the salt, pepper and garlic over the asparagus, then stir the cornflour into the sour cream, pour it over the asparagus and spread to the edges of the dish.

Sprinkle the breadcrumbs and tarragon over the sour cream and place small pieces of butter over the breadcrumbs. Bake for 15–20 minutes.

45 minutes to make
Good source of vitamin A, B group vitamins, vitamin C

Aubergine Casserole

Serve with a green vegetable or salad.

1 large aubergine
2oz/55g butter or margarine
1 large or 2 medium onions
2 cloves garlic, crushed
1lb/455g mushrooms, sliced
6 courgettes, sliced
1 × 14oz/397g tin chopped tomatoes
salt and freshly ground black pepper to taste
1 teaspoon chopped fresh oregano
1 tablespoon breadcrumbs
4 tablespoons Parmesan cheese, grated

Pre-heat the oven to 350°F/180°C (Gas Mark 4) and lightly oil a casserole dish. Peel and cube the aubergine, then cover it with boiling water and simmer for 10 minutes. Drain well.

Melt the butter in a frying pan and sauté the onion and garlic for 4–5 minutes until soft. Add the mushrooms, courgettes and aubergine and continue to cook for 10 minutes, stirring often.

Mix the tomatoes, salt, pepper and oregano together in a small saucepan and simmer gently for 10 minutes.

Spoon some of the tomato sauce into the casserole dish. Then place on top a layer of aubergine and mushroom mixture, followed by another layer of tomato sauce, and so on until both mixtures are used up. Sprinkle the top with Parmesan and breadcrumbs, cover and bake for 40 minutes, removing the lid for the last 10 minutes to brown the top lightly.

1 hour 15 minutes to make
Good source of vitamin A, B group vitamins, vitamin C, potassium

Beefless Rice Casserole

As with all dishes including TVP, this is both easier and quicker to make than a beef casserole that uses butcher's meat. Choose beef-flavoured TVP chunks if you want to keep a beef-type taste. If you use vegetable burgers instead, do remember to reduce the amount of liquid you use.

1½fl.oz/45ml vegetable oil
1 stick celery, chopped
1 large onion, chopped
8oz/225g white rice
1 × 4½oz/128g packet TVP chunks, or 4 vegetable burgers, cubed
8fl.oz/230ml vegetable stock or water (4fl.oz if using vegetable burgers)
2 × 14oz/397g tins chopped tomatoes
1 tablespoon soy sauce
salt and freshly ground black pepper to taste
1 teaspoon chilli powder (optional)
1 teaspoon mixed herbs (optional)

Pre-heat the oven to 325°F/170°C (Gas Mark 3) and lightly grease a casserole dish. Heat the oil in a saucepan and sauté the celery and onion until just tender.

Add the rice and TVP chunks, and stir for a few minutes until the chunks are slightly browned. Now add the vegetable stock, tomatoes, soy sauce, salt pepper and optional seasonings if desired. Stir well and bring to the boil.

Remove the mixture from the heat and pour into the casserole dish. Bake, covered, for 30 minutes.

40 minutes to make
Good source of protein, vitamin A, vitamin C

Beefless Stew

Serve with mashed potatoes or rice, and green vegetables or a salad.

1 large onion, chopped
4 medium carrots, chopped
4 medium potatoes, cubed
2 cloves garlic, crushed
2 sticks celery, chopped
½ red pepper, chopped and deseeded
2oz/55g butter or margarine
1 × 4½oz/128g packet TVP chunks or 4 vegetable burgers, cubed
1 × 14oz/397g tin chopped tomatoes
1 pint/570ml vegetable stock or water (½ pint if using vegetable burgers)
2 tablespoons soy sauce
salt and freshly ground black pepper to taste

Prepare the vegetables, then melt the butter in a large saucepan and lightly brown the onion. Add the other vegetables and sauté for a few minutes. Then add the TVP chunks and brown for 3 minutes over a gentle heat. Add the tomatoes and enough vegetable stock just to cover the mixture.

Season with soy sauce, salt and pepper, cover the stew and simmer for 30–40 minutes or until thick and well cooked. Take care to add extra vegetable stock or water if the mixture seems dry.

55 minutes to make
Good source of vitamin A, B group vitamins, calcium, potassium

Beefless Stroganoff

Serve with rice and green vegetables or a salad. As a variation to this warming dish, put the whole vegetable burgers in the bottom of a casserole and warm through. Cover with the sauce.

2oz/55g butter or margarine
1 large onion, chopped
12oz/340g mushrooms, sliced
1 teaspoon paprika
1oz/25g plain flour
6 vegetable burgers, cubed
6fl.oz/180ml white wine
a little vegetable stock or water
3fl.oz/90ml sour cream
½ teaspoon mild mustard

Melt the butter in a pan, and fry the onions and mushrooms, with the paprika, for 10 minutes. Add the flour and the cubed vegetable burgers, stir well and brown for 2 minutes.

Pour in the wine and and simmer very gently for 10–15 minutes. Stir often and add a little vegetable stock if the mixture seems dry.

Finally, add the sour cream and mustard, then heat through but do not boil or simmer. Serve immediately.

25 minutes to make
Good source of vitamin A, B group vitamins

Burgers Bourguignonne

Serve with potatoes and green vegetables or a salad. Remember to reduce the liquid if using vegetable burgers rather than TVP chunks.

2oz/55g butter or margarine
10 small onions, peeled
5 medium carrots, chopped
6 large mushrooms, chopped
1 stick celery, chopped
1 × 4½oz/128g packet TVP chunks or 6 vegetable burgers, cubed
2 teaspoons plain flour
12fl.oz/340ml vegetable stock or water (6fl.oz if using vegetable burgers)
1 tablespoon tomato puree
1 teaspoon vegetable extract or soy sauce
4fl.oz/120ml red wine
1 bay leaf
2 cloves garlic, crushed or 1 teaspoon garlic powder
3 tablespoons chopped fresh parsley
1 teaspoon chopped fresh thyme
salt and freshly ground black pepper to taste

Melt the butter in a large saucepan, add the onions and sauté for 2–3 minutes. Add the remaining vegetables and sauté them for 5–6 minutes, stirring often. Add the TVP chunks to the sauté and brown for 3 minutes over a low heat.

Mix the flour into a paste using a little of the vegetable stock. Add this paste, the tomato puree and the yeast extract to the sauté.

Stir in the remaining vegetable stock and the wine, bay leaf, garlic and herbs. Reduce the heat, cover, and simmer for 30–40 minutes until the chunks are tender and the flavours well developed. Season to taste with the salt and pepper.

55 minutes to make
Good source of vitamin A, B group vitamins, calcium, iron

Burgers in Sour Cream and Red Wine

Serve with rice, pasta, and green vegetables or a salad.

3oz/85g butter or margarine
1 clove garlic, crushed
6 vegetable burgers
2 medium onions, chopped
8oz/225g carrots, chopped
4 sticks celery, chopped
4fl.oz/120ml red wine
4fl.oz/120ml vegetable stock or water
2 bay leaves
3 tablespoons chopped fresh parsley
salt and freshly ground black pepper to taste
1 tablespoon chopped fresh thyme or 1 teaspoon dried thyme
12fl.oz/340ml sour cream
1 teaspoon paprika
1 tablespoon soy sauce

Pre-heat the oven to 350°F/180°C (Gas Mark 4) and lightly grease a casserole dish. Melt the butter in a saucepan and sauté the garlic. Then add the burgers and brown them on both sides, for about 5 minutes. Put the burgers in the casserole dish.

Add the onions to the hot fat and sauté until tender, then add the chopped carrot and celery and sauté for a further 5 minutes.

Add the remaining ingredients – except the sour cream, paprika and soy sauce – and stir gently for 5 minutes. Pour this mixture over the burgers in the casserole. Cover, and bake for 1 hour.

Just before serving, stir in the sour cream, paprika and soy sauce.

1 hour 30 minutes to make
Good source of vitamin A, vitamin C, calcium

Festive or Sunday Roast with Savoury Stuffing (p. 20)

Greek Beefless Stew (p. 91)

Shepherd's Pie (p. 54)

Sunday Breakfast (p. 69)

Cheese and Noodle Casserole

1lb/455g noodles
8fl.oz/230ml sour cream
1 × 12oz/340g packet cream cheese (or soft cheese)
8oz/225g cottage cheese
8 tablespoons milk
2 tablespoons chopped chives
salt and freshly ground black pepper to taste
up to 1 tablespoon chopped fresh herbs (e.g. marjoram) or 1 teaspoon caraway seeds
1oz/25g butter or margarine
1 tablespoon chopped fresh parsley
2oz/55g Parmesan cheese, grated

Pre-heat the oven to 350°F/180°C (Gas Mark 4) and lightly grease a baking dish. Boil the noodles, rinse under cold water, drain and put to one side.

In a large mixing bowl combine the sour cream, cream cheese, cottage cheese and milk. Add the noodles and toss gently. Add the chives, salt, pepper and herbs or caraway seeds, and stir well. Then tip the mixture into the baking dish and dab pieces of butter over the top.

Sprinkle the parsley and Parmesan over the dish and bake, uncovered, for 30 minutes. Serve hot.

45 minutes to make
Good source of protein, vitamin A, B group vitamins, calcium

Cheese and Tomato Casserole

8 tomatoes
2oz/55g butter or margarine
1 small onion, chopped
1½oz/45g plain flour
1 pint/570ml milk
salt and freshly ground black pepper to taste
1/2 teaspoon paprika
2 egg yolks, beaten
2 tablespoons double cream
4oz/115g Swiss cheese, grated

for the garnish:
1 tablespoon freshly chopped parsley or tarragon

Pre-heat the oven to 350°F/180°C (Gas Mark 4) and lightly grease a casserole dish. Quickly plunge the tomatoes into boiling water, then into cold water, then skin them. Cut them into thick slices and arrange them in the casserole dish.

Melt the butter in a large saucepan and sauté the onions until tender. Reduce the heat, and sprinkle the flour over the onions, stirring to make a thick paste.

Heat the milk in a separate pan and add it gradually to the paste, stirring constantly to make a smooth sauce. Add the salt, pepper and paprika. Stir well then allow the sauce to cool for a couple of minutes.

Mix the egg yolks with the cream. Add these to the sauce, stirring over a very low heat. Add the cheese, and stir as it melts.

Pour the sauce over the tomatoes and bake, uncovered, for 15–20 minutes. Sprinkle the fresh herbs over the cooked dish and serve immediately.

35 minutes to make
Good source of protein, vitamin A, B group vitamins, vitamin C

Chilli non Carne

The best chilli you'll get this side of Tijuana! Serve with rice, mashed potatoes or avocado salad.

2 tablespoons vegetable oil
1 medium onion, chopped
1½ level teaspoons chilli powder (or more according to taste)
2 × 4½oz/128g packets TVP chunks or 4 vegetable burgers, crumbled
12–15fl.oz/340–430ml vegetable stock or water (6fl.oz if using vegetable burgers)
1 × 14oz/397g tin chopped tomatoes
1 × 14oz/397g tin red kidney beans
2 Mexican green chillies in brine, drained and chopped (optional)
salt and freshly ground black pepper to taste

Heat the oil in a large saucepan and sauté the onion until golden brown. Add the chilli powder and TVP chunks and brown for 5 minutes.

Add the vegetable stock and tomatoes, together with their juice. Cover the mixture and simmer for 20 minutes.

Add the kidney beans – and the chillies if you are using them – and simmer for about 15 minutes, adding a little extra stock or water if necessary. Season to taste and serve hot.

45 minutes to make
Good source of protein, vitamin A, vitamin C

Ghivetch Casserole

A friend gave me this recipe. It should be served with rice or pasta.

3 tablespoons olive oil
2 onions, chopped
2 cloves garlic, crushed
5oz/140g marrow, cubed
2 medium carrots, sliced
3oz/85g mushrooms, halved if large
5oz/140g courgettes, sliced
½ medium cauliflower, or 1 small cauliflower, broken into florets
1 small aubergine, cubed
1 green pepper, deseeded and roughly chopped
2 sticks celery, chopped
2 potatoes, diced
8oz/225g broad beans or sweetcorn
8oz/225g peas or green beans
juice of ½ lemon
8fl.oz/230ml vegetable stock
1 × 14oz/397g tin tomatoes
2 tablespoons tomato puree (optional)
1 teaspoon chopped dill
salt and freshly ground black pepper to taste

Pre-heat the oven to 350°F/180°C (Gas Mark 4). Heat the oil in a very large pan and sauté the onion and garlic for 3–4 minutes. Then add the remaining vegetables and mix well. Cook, covered tightly, for 5 minutes to bring out the flavour.

Add the remaining ingredients to the vegetables and pour the mixture into a large casserole dish. Bake for 1 hour, stirring the casserole twice during that time. Season to taste.

1 hour 25 minutes to make
Good source of vitamin A, B group vitamins, vitamin C, potassium

Greek Beefless Stew

2oz/55g butter or margarine
6 vegetable burgers, cubed
12 small onions or 4 medium onions, chopped
2 tablespoons tomato puree
15fl.oz/430ml vegetable stock or water
4 carrots, chopped
2 medium potatoes, chopped
1 teaspoon ground cinnamon
salt and freshly ground black pepper to taste

Melt the butter in a frying pan, brown the burger chunks for about 5 minutes, then place them in a deep stew pot or saucepan. Arrange the onions on top.

Add the tomato puree to the remaining hot fat in the frying pan and stir well. Gradually add the vegetable stock, stir well and bring this mixture to the boil. Pour the sauce over the onions and burger chunks, add the carrots, potatoes, cinnamon, salt and pepper and stir well. Add a little more liquid if necessary.

Cover the pot and cook for 40–45 minutes over a low heat. Serve immediately in bowls. Have plenty of fresh bread on hand.

1 hour to make
Good source of vitamin A, vitamin C

Italian Burgers

Serve hot with rice, pasta or potatoes and a green salad.

2 tablespoons olive oil
6 vegetable burgers
1 large onion, chopped
2 cloves garlic, crushed
2 × 14oz/397g tins chopped tomatoes
1 tablespoon freshly chopped oregano or basil or 1 tablespoon dried
salt and freshly ground black pepper to taste
16 black olives, stoned and chopped (optional)
4oz/115g Mozzarella cheese, sliced

Pre-heat the oven to 350°F/ 180°C (Gas Mark 4). Heat the oil in a frying pan and brown the burgers on both sides, about 5 minutes in total. Then remove them from the pan and put to one side.

Sauté the onion and garlic in the hot oil until tender, then add the tomatoes, oregano and seasoning. Simmer for 15 minutes to thicken.

Put the burgers in a casserole dish. Place the olives on top and pour the sauce over them. Cover with slices of Mozzarella and bake for 30 minutes.

55 minutes to make
Good source of protein, vitamin A, vitamin C, calcium

Lentil and Steaklets Stew

Serves 6–8.

1 large onion, chopped
2 sticks celery, chopped
1 clove garlic, crushed
1 bay leaf
3 pints/1.7l vegetable stock or water (1½ pints if using vegetable burgers)
1 × 14oz/397g tin chopped tomatoes
1 × 4½ oz/128g packet TVP chunks or 4 vegetable burgers, cubed
8oz/225g lentils
2oz/55g macaroni
1 teaspoon dried thyme
1 teaspoon dried oregano
salt and freshly ground black pepper to taste

In a large saucepan combine the onion, celery, garlic, bay leaf, vegetable stock, tomatoes and TVP chunks. Cover tightly and simmer for 30 minutes over a medium heat.

Wash the lentils twice in cold water. Drain them well.

Stir the lentils, macaroni, thyme, oregano, salt and pepper into the stew. Cover, and cook for 25 minutes. Serve hot.

1 hour 10 minutes to make
Good source of protein, vitamin A, vitamin C, iron

Madras Onion Curry

Serve with rice and condiments such as nuts, grated coconut and chutneys.

3 tablespoons vegetable oil
1 large onion, chopped
1 clove garlic, crushed
1 tablespoon curry powder
1 × 4½oz/128g packet TVP chunks or 4 vegetable burgers, cubed
1 small apple
15fl.oz/430ml vegetable stock or water (10fl.oz if using vegetable burgers)
1 tablespoon soy sauce
1 teaspoon grated lemon rind
1 tablespoon brown sugar
salt and freshly ground black pepper to taste
¼ teaspoon ground ginger
2 tablespoons cornflour
2 tablespoons cold water

Heat the vegetable oil in a large saucepan and sauté the onion, garlic and curry powder until lightly browned.

Add the TVP chunks or cubed vegetable burgers to the mixture and stir for 5 minutes over a low heat.

Peel, core and chop the apple and add it to the sauté. Now add the remaining ingredients (except the cornflour and cold water). Stir well, cover the pan, and simmer for 10 minutes.

Mix the cornflour and cold water together in a small bowl. Add this mixture to the curry and simmer, stirring often, until the sauce thickens. Leave to cook, uncovered, for a further 5 minutes.

30 minutes to make

Mince and Aubergine Casserole

3 medium aubergines
2oz/55g butter or margarine
1 large onion, chopped
1 medium green pepper, chopped (optional)
half a 4½oz/128g packet TVP mince (or 2 vegetable burgers, crumbled)
1 tablespoon plain flour
2 × 14oz/397g tins chopped tomatoes
1 × 5oz/140g tin tomato puree
1 teaspoon dried oregano
salt and freshly ground black pepper to taste
½ pint/290ml vegetable stock (optional)
6oz/170g Cheddar cheese, grated

Pre-heat the oven to 350°F/180°C (Gas Mark 4) and lightly grease a casserole dish. Peel the aubergine using a potato peeler and cut into strips.

Cook the aubergine strips for 5 minutes in boiling water until they are tender, then drain them. Melt the butter in a large saucepan and sauté the onion and green pepper for 2–3 minutes. Add the TVP mince and stir over a low heat for about 3 minutes. Add the flour and cook for 2 minutes longer.

Stir in the tomatoes, tomato puree, oregano and seasoning. Allow to simmer for 5 minutes, stirring occasionally. Add a little vegetable stock or water if a moist sauce is desired.

Spread a layer of aubergine on the bottom of the casserole dish. Add a layer of the mince/tomato mixture, and then a layer of grated cheese. Alternate these layers until all the ingredients are used. End with a layer of cheese. Bake, uncovered, for 30 minutes, until the cheese makes a golden crust.

55 minutes to make
Good source of protein, vitamin A, vitamin C, calcium

Oriental Beefless Casserole

1oz/25g butter or margarine
1 large onion, chopped
4 sticks celery, chopped
2 cloves garlic, crushed or 1 teaspoon garlic powder
2 teaspoons grated fresh root ginger
half a 4½oz/128g packet TVP mince
4oz/115g long grain rice
24fl.oz/690ml tomato juice
4 tablespoons soy sauce

Pre-heat the oven to 350°F/180°C (Gas Mark 4) and lightly grease a casserole dish. Melt the butter in a saucepan and sauté the onions, celery, garlic and ginger until light brown.

Add the TVP mince and stir together for 3–4 minutes. Spoon half of this mixture into the casserole dish and cover with the uncooked rice.

Place the remaining onion and celery mixture over the rice. Blend the tomato juice and soy sauce together and pour over the casserole.

Bake, covered, for 30 minutes.

45 minutes to make
Good source of vitamin A, calcium

Sour Cream Steaklet Chunks

Serve with potatoes or rice or pasta and green vegetables.

2 tablespoons vegetable oil
1 large onion, chopped
1 teaspoon thyme
1 bay leaf
salt and freshly ground black pepper to taste
1 × 4½oz/128g packet TVP chunks or 6 vegetable burgers, cubed
8fl.oz/230ml tomato juice
8fl.oz/230ml water or vegetable stock (if using TVP chunks)
10oz/285g frozen peas
5fl.oz/140ml sour cream
1 teaspoon horseradish sauce

Heat the oil in a large saucepan and sauté the onion. Add the thyme, bay leaf and seasoning. Stir well.

Add the TVP chunks and tomato juice (and vegetable stock too, if using TVP chunks), cover the pan and simmer gently for 30 minutes until the chunks are tender.

Add the peas and a little extra vegetable stock if necessary, and simmer for 5 minutes. Then stir in the sour cream and horseradish sauce. Serve immediately.

45 minutes to make
Good source of vitamin A, B group vitamins, vitamin C

Tomatoes Provençal and Mince

Good to eat with fresh vegetables, salad or hot rice.

6 large tomatoes
6 tablespoons olive oil
1oz/25g butter or margarine
1 medium onion, chopped
1 clove garlic, crushed
8 vegetable burgers
½oz/15g plain flour
15fl.oz/430ml vegetable stock or water
salt and freshly ground black pepper to taste
2 tablespoons chopped fresh parsley

Pre-heat the oven to 400°F/200°C (Gas Mark 6). Halve the tomatoes and place them in a frying pan with the oil, cut side down. Cook for 5 minutes over a medium heat. Pierce the tomato skins with a fork and peel the skins off as they warm. Remove the tomatoes onto a plate.

Melt the butter in the frying pan and sauté the onions and garlic until lightly browned. Crumble the burgers into the sauté and stir well.

Now sprinkle the flour over the sauté and stir to thicken the sauce. Gradually add the vegetable stock, stirring constantly, and cook over a medium heat until this also thickens.

Add the salt, pepper and most of the parsley to the sauté. Stir well and pour the mixture into a casserole dish. Arrange the tomatoes on top, sprinkle the remaining parsley over the tomatoes and bake the casserole, uncovered, for 15 minutes. Serve immediately.

30 minutes to make
Good source of protein, vitamin A, vitamin C

Vegetable Burger Stew with Tomatoes, Peas and Cheese Topping

Serve hot with rice.

3 tablespoons vegetable oil
2 tablespoons chopped shallots or onion
1oz/25g butter or margarine
6 vegetable burgers, cubed
salt and freshly ground black pepper to taste
1×14oz/397g tin chopped tomatoes
1 teaspoon mixed dried herbs
1 bay leaf
2lb/910g fresh peas or 10oz/285g frozen petits pois

for the garnish:
3oz/85g Cheddar cheese, grated

Heat the oil in a frying pan and sauté the onion until lightly browned. Melt the butter in a separate saucepan and brown the burger chunks (about 5 minutes in total).

Mix the onions and burger chunks together and add all the remaining ingredients except the peas and grated cheese. Stir well.

Cover the pan and simmer the mixture for 20 minutes, adding a little vegetable stock or water if necessary to keep the mixture moist.

Add the peas and cook for a further 10 minutes. Serve hot over rice and garnish with grated cheese.

45 minutes to make
Good source of protein, vitamin A, vitamin C, calcium

Vegetable Burger Supreme

Serve with rice, vegetables or noodles.

    2 tablespoons olive oil
    6 vegetable burgers
    1oz/25g butter or margarine
    1 medium onion, chopped
    2 cloves garlic, crushed
    salt and freshly ground black pepper to taste
    4 tablespoons white wine
    4 tablespoons sherry
    4 tablespoons vegetable stock or water
    2 egg yolks
    2 tablespoons double cream
    2 tablespoons chopped fresh parsley

Heat the oil in a frying pan and brown the burgers over a medium heat for about 5 minutes, turning often. Remove from the heat.

Melt the butter in the frying pan and sauté the onion and garlic until lightly browned. Add the seasoning.

Stir in the wine, sherry and stock and simmer for 3–4 minutes. Whisk the egg yolks and double cream together in a small bowl.

Pour the cream mixture into the wine sauce and stir well. Add the parsley, then the browned burgers, and bring up to a simmer. Serve hot.

30 minutes to make
Good source of protein, vitamin A

Vegetable Burgers in White Wine

Serve with fresh vegetables, rice or mashed pota-toes. As a variation, you could use 1 tablespoon of fresh (or 1 teaspoon dried) rosemary in place of the dill weed.

2oz/55g butter or margarine
6 vegetable burgers
1½lb/680g mushrooms, sliced
1oz/25g plain flour
12fl.oz/340ml vegetable stock or water
12fl.oz/340ml white wine
½ teaspoon dried dill weed
salt and freshly ground black pepper to taste

Pre-heat the oven to 350°F/180°C (Gas Mark 4). Melt the butter in a large frying pan and brown the burgers (about 5 minutes in total). Remove them on to a plate and keep them warm in the oven.

Sauté the mushrooms in the remaining butter until tender.

Sprinkle the flour over this sauté and stir well to make a thick paste. Gradually add the stock and the wine to make a smooth, thick sauce. Add the dill weed and stir constantly over a low heat for 4–5 minutes. Season well, and pour the sauce over the burgers. Serve hot.

30 minutes to make
Good source of protein, B group vitamins, potassium

Vegetable Curry

1½oz/45g butter or margarine
1 large onion, chopped
6 medium potatoes, chopped
1 apple, peeled and chopped
1 turnip, chopped
3 leeks, thinly sliced
4 medium carrots, thinly sliced
6 sticks celery, thinly sliced
4 tablespoons mild curry powder (or to taste)
1 tablespoon brown sugar
2 tablespoons soy sauce
1 × 4½oz/128g packet TVP chunks or 4 vegetable burgers, cubed
1 pint/570ml water or vegetable stock

Melt the butter in a large soup pan over a medium heat. Add the vegetables and toss them in the butter for a few minutes. Then add the curry powder, sugar, soy sauce and TVP chunks and stir well. Cover the mixture with water.

Cover the pan and cook over a medium heat until the vegetables are tender. Stir the curry occasionally, but otherwise keep the pan covered. Serve immediately, although this dish will benefit from standing for an hour or so before being either reheated or served cold.

45 minutes to make
Good source of protein, vitamin A, vitamin C, potassium

Vegetables and Baked Schnitzels in White Wine

1oz/25g butter or margarine
6 vegetable schnitzels or vegetable burgers
2 onions, chopped
6oz/170g carrots, thinly sliced
2 sticks celery, thinly sliced
salt and freshly ground black pepper to taste
8fl.oz/230ml vegetable stock or water
8fl.oz/230ml white wine

Pre-heat the oven to 375°F/190°C (Gas Mark 5).

Melt the butter in a frying pan and brown the schnitzels on both sides (about 5 minutes in total).

Mix the prepared vegetables in an oven-to-table casserole dish, and place the browned schnitzels on top. Sprinkle the salt and pepper over the schnitzels and pour the vegetable stock and white wine over them.

Bake the casserole, uncovered, until most of the liquid has evaporated (about 45–60 minutes). Check it from time to time and baste the schnitzels with the liquid. Serve hot, straight from the casserole dish.

1 hour 15 minutes to make
Good source of protein, vitamin A, B group vitamins, potassium

VEGETABLE
SPECIALITIES

Breaded Broccoli

1½lb/680g broccoli
1½oz/45g butter or margarine
3oz/85g fresh breadcrumbs
salt and freshly ground black pepper to taste
1 tablespoon lemon juice

Trim the thick stems from the broccoli and steam the heads until tender.

Melt the butter in a saucepan, add the bread-crumbs and fry until crisp. Sprinkle in the salt and pepper and stir.

Place the cooked broccoli in a warm serving dish, pour the lemon juice over, then sprinkle with the breadcrumb mixture and serve immediately.

15 minutes to make
Good source of vitamin A, B group vitamins, vitamin C

Carrot and Turnip Puree

Serve hot as a side dish, or as a filling in baked potatoes.

6–8 medium carrots, cubed
1 small white turnip, cubed
1–2oz/25–55g butter or margarine
salt and freshly ground black pepper to taste

Place the carrots and turnip in a pan, barely cover with water and boil until tender.

Put the cooked vegetables in a food processor and puree with the butter, salt and pepper until soft and smooth. Alternatively, mash them by hand. Serve hot.

30 minutes to make
Good source of vitamin A, B group vitamins, vitamin C, potassium

Fried Rice

This is a little bit different from the usual recipes for fried rice. I find that it makes a great dish all by itself, and is extremely adaptable – you can also serve it with a selection of vegetables.

12oz/340g long grain rice
2 tablespoons vegetable oil
1 medium onion, chopped
2 sticks celery, chopped
8oz/225g mushrooms, chopped
2–3 tablespoons soy sauce
2 eggs, beaten
2 spring onions, chopped
1 tomato, chopped

Cover the rice with twice its volume of water (i.e. 1 cup of rice to 2 cups water) in a medium-sized saucepan. Bring to a boil, then cover the pan, reduce the heat and leave the rice to simmer for about 20 minutes or until all the water is absorbed.

Heat the oil in a large pan and sauté the onion, celery and mushrooms for about 5 minutes. Add the cooked rice and the soy sauce, then stir for about 3 minutes.

Add the eggs to the rice mixture, stirring as it cooks, about 5 minutes.

Add the spring onions and tomatoes and cook for a final 5 minutes.

50 minutes to make
Good source of vitamin A, vitamin C

Glazed Carrots

1lb/455g carrots, sliced
1oz/25g butter or margarine
1–2 tablespoons brown sugar
½ teaspoon ground ginger

Steam or boil the carrots until tender. Drain them.

Melt the butter in a frying pan over a low flame. Stir the sugar and ginger into the melted butter until the sugar is dissolved. This will make a light brown glaze.

Add the sliced carrots to the pan and stir gently but continuously until all the carrots are glazed and hot. Serve immediately.

20 minutes to make
Good source of vitamin A

Harvard Beets

2lb/910g beetroot
2 teaspoons cornflour
2oz/55g sugar
8fl.oz/230ml cider vinegar
2fl.oz/60ml water
1oz/25g butter or margarine

Wash the beetroot (do not trim its 'tail' yet) and boil until tender. Drain, trim and slice the beetroot and place to one side.

Combine the cornflour and sugar in a saucepan. Stir the vinegar and water into it and cook over a low heat until the sauce is thick. Stir constantly.

Add the sliced beetroot and the butter to the sauce and stir gently until the butter melts. Serve immediately.

30 minutes to make

Jerusalem Artichokes in Lemon Parsley Sauce

1lb/455g Jerusalem artichokes, peeled
2oz/55g butter or margarine
3 tablespoons chopped fresh parsley or parsley and chives
2 tablespoons lemon juice
salt and freshly ground black pepper to taste

Boil the artichokes for 20–25 minutes, until tender.

Drain the artichokes and puree them in a blender or mash them in the pan. Add the butter, stirring well as it melts, then the parsley, lemon juice, salt and pepper.

Mix very well and serve immediately.

40 minutes to make
Good source of vitamin A, vitamin C

Mushrooms and Rice

4 tablespoons vegetable oil
8oz/225g mushrooms, finely chopped
8oz/225g long grain rice
1 pint/570ml vegetable stock or water
sprig of tarragon or other herb for flavouring

Heat the oil in a saucepan and brown the mush-rooms over a medium heat for about 5 minutes.

Add the rice and vegetable stock, and flavour with the herb. Cover the pan, reduce the heat and simmer for about 20 minutes, until the water has been absorbed. Serve immediately.

25 minutes to make
Good source of vitamin A, B group vitamins

Mushroom Risotto

2oz/55g butter or margarine
2 medium onions, chopped
8oz/225g mushrooms, chopped
8oz/225g white rice
1 pint/570ml boiling vegetable stock or water
salt and freshly ground black pepper to taste
1oz/25g Parmesan cheese
1oz/25g butter or margarine, melted

Melt the butter in a deep saucepan, and sauté the onions for 5 minutes, until tender. Then add the mushrooms, and cook gently for 10 minutes.

Add the rice to the pan and cook for about 5 minutes, until it begins to go clear.

Add the vegetable stock, salt and pepper and bring the mixture to a simmer, stirring all the while. Then reduce the heat, cover the pan and leave it to cook for 15–20 minutes, until the liquid is absorbed.

Remove the lid, sprinkle the cheese over the top and pour the melted butter over that. Serve immediately.

35 minutes to make
Good source of vitamin A, B group vitamins

Mushrooms and Onions in Sherry

Serve over rice or mashed potatoes.

2oz/55g butter or margarine
1 medium onion, chopped
1lb/455g mushrooms, sliced
2 tablespoons plain flour
4 tablespoons chopped fresh parsley
6fl.oz/180ml vegetable stock or water
2fl.oz/60ml sherry or brandy
salt and freshly ground black pepper to taste

Melt the butter in a saucepan and sauté the onions until soft. Add the mushrooms and cook them until they begin to release their juices. Sprinkle the flour over the sauté and cook for 1 minute, stirring constantly.

Add the parsley and stock, and stir over a low heat until the mushrooms are tender and the sauce has thickened.

Add the sherry or brandy, increase the heat and cook for a further 5 minutes. Season to taste. Serve immediately.

20 minutes to make
Good source of B group vitamins

New Orleans Broad Beans

People who were once put off the taste of badly-prepared broad beans will be tempted back again to this southern recipe, which can be served to accompany just about any main course.

1lb/455g broad beans
2 tablespoons olive oil
1 medium onion, chopped
1 small green or red pepper, chopped
2 sticks celery, chopped
1 × 14oz/397g tin chopped tomatoes
1 tablespoon sugar (or to taste)
salt and freshly ground black pepper to taste

Boil the beans until tender (about 7 minutes). Drain them and set aside. Heat the oil in a saucepan and gently sauté the onions, pepper and celery for 5–6 minutes until lightly browned.

Add the tomatoes and the sugar, stir well and simmer for 20 minutes, uncovered.

Add the beans and season to taste. Bring the mixture back to a simmer and cook for a further 5 minutes. Serve immediately.

40 minutes to make
Good source of B group vitamins, vitamin C, potassium

Orange and Beetroot

6 medium beetroot (approx. 1lb/455g)
4fl.oz/120ml water
4fl.oz/120ml orange juice
2 teaspoons grated orange rind
1 tablespoon cider vinegar or rice vinegar or wine vinegar
1 tablespoon brown sugar
2 tablespoons cornflour
2oz/55g butter or margarine
pinch of nutmeg
salt and freshly ground black pepper to taste

Cook the beetroot in boiling water for 20 minutes. Remove from the heat but leave them in the boiled water to keep hot.

Mix the remaining ingredients together in a saucepan. Bring to the boil and simmer, stirring, for about 25 minutes until the cornflour has cooked and the sauce is clear.

Peel and cube the hot beetroot and place in a warm serving dish. Pour the sauce over the hot beetroot and serve immediately.

40 minutes to make
Good source of vitamin C

Pureed Parsnips

A great favourite – serve with any main course and green vegetable.

6 medium parsnips, peeled and cubed
1oz/25g butter or margarine
2 tablespoons milk
salt and freshly ground black pepper to taste

Boil the parsnips until tender (about 20 minutes). Drain.

Place the parsnips in a blender with the butter, milk, salt and pepper and puree to a smooth, light consistency. Serve hot.

25 minutes to make
Good source of vitamin C

Refried Beans

Used in many Mexican recipes, a great filling for tacos.

1lb/455g dried pinto beans, washed and drained
2 pints/1.1l water
2 medium onions, chopped
7fl.oz/205ml vegetable oil or 7oz/200g vegetable suet
salt and freshly ground black pepper to taste

Measure the beans and water into a large saucepan and place over a high heat. Bring the water to the boil, cover the pan, turn off the heat and let the beans soak for 1½ hours.

Add the onions to the beans. Bring the liquid to a boil again, then reduce the heat and simmer, covered, until the beans are very tender, for about 2½–3 hours. Replace any water that is lost through evaporation. (If you want to save time here, use a pressure cooker to cook the beans.)

When the beans are very soft, mash them up (or use a blender) and add the vegetable oil, salt and pepper. Serve hot or cold.

3 hours 45 minutes to make
Good source of protein, B group vitamins, potassium, iron

Sauerkraut

2lb/910g white cabbage, finely shredded
4oz/115g coarse sea salt
2 pints/1.1l cider vinegar
2 teaspoons caraway seeds
5 teaspoons whole pickling spice
3 bay leaves

Cover the bottom of a very large mixing bowl with shredded cabbage and sprinkle a layer of salt over it. Continue to layer the cabbage and salt in this way until all the cabbage is used. Make sure that a layer of salt covers the top layer of cabbage.

Cover the bowl with a towel and then a large plate and leave to stand for 12–24 hours. (If you make this one evening, you may finish it the next evening.)

Mix the vinegar and spices together in an enamel pan and bring to a soft boil. Cover the pan and remove it from the heat. Leave this mixture to stand undisturbed for 12–24 hours also.

Drain the cabbage and rinse it very well in cold water to remove the salt. Then pack the cabbage into sterile jars and pour the cool vinegar mixture over until the cabbage is covered. Seal the jars and keep in a cool place until ready to use.

24 hours to make

Index

Asparagus and Egg
  Casserole 78—9
Asparagus Casserole with
  Sour Cream 80
Asparagus in Divine
  Sauce 1
Asparagus with Cheese 2
Aubergine and Pasta 3
Aubergine Caponata 4
Aubergine Casserole 81
Aubergine Parmigiano 5
Baked Macaroni Cheese 6
Baked Sweetcorn 7
Beefless Pie 8
Beefless Rice Casserole 82
Beefless Stew 83
Beefless Stroganoff 84
Beer Fondue 9
Breaded Broccoli 104
Burgers Bourguignonne
  85
Burgers in Sour Cream
  and Red Wine 86
Carrot and Turnip Puree
  105
Cauliflower Mexican Style
  10
Cheddar Cheese Bake 11
Cheddar Cheese Pie 12
Cheese and Noodle
  Casserole 87
Cheese and Tomato
  Casserole 88
Cheese Soufflé 13
Cheese with Herbs and
  Pasta 14
Chilli non Carne 89
Corn Soufflé 15
Cottage Cheese Pie 16
Curried Lentils 17
Eggs au Gratin 18
Eggs Florentine 19
Festive or Sunday Roast
  with Savoury Stuffing
  21
French Baked Eggs 22
Fried Rice 106
Glazed Carrots 107
Ghivetch Casserole 90
Gnocchi 23
Greek Beefless Stew 91

Green Chilli and Rice 24
Harvard Beets 108
Hearts of Artichoke with
  Mushroom Sauce 25
Herby Cheese and Rice
  Bowl 26
Hot Dogs and Tomatoes
  27
Italian Burgers 92
Jerusalem Artichokes in
  Lemon Parsley Sauce
  109
Lasagne Italiano 28
Lentil and Steaklets Stew
  93
Lentil Cheese Loaf 29
Linda's Lasagne 30
Madras Onion Curry 94
Maine Sauerkraut 31
Meatless Loaf 32
Meatless Loaf with Herbs
  33
Mexican Corn Pudding 34
Mexican Loaf 35
Mince and Aubergine
  Casserole 95
Moussaka 36–7
Mushroom Loaf 38
Mushroom Pie 39
Mushroom Risotto 111
Mushrooms and Onions
  in Sherry 112
Mushrooms and Rice 110
New Orleans Broad Beans
  113
Olive and Steaklet Bake
  40
Orange and Beetroot 114
Oriental Beefless
  Casserole 96
Penne with Vodka 41
Pepper Steaklets 42
Peruvian Burgers 43
Potato Torte á la Faranto
  44
Pureed Parsnips 115
Refried Beans 116
Rice and Beans 46
Rice and Vegetables in
  Wine 47
Rice in Tasty Vegetable
  Stock 48

Rice with Asparagus 49
Sauerkraut 117
Sauté Schnitzel 50
Savoury Rice 51
Savoury Turnovers 52
Schnitzel Scaloppini in
  White Wine 53
Shepherd's Pie 54
Simple Beefless Hash 55
Sour Cream Soufflé 56
Sour Cream, Paprika and
  Mushrooms 57
Sour Cream Steaklet
  Chunks 97
Spaghetti Omlette 58
Spanish Burgers 59
Spanish Omelette 60
Spicy Eggs 61
Spinach and Sour Cream
  Omelette 62
Spinach Cheese
  Dumplings 63
Spinach Pie 64
Steaklets Diane 65
Steaklets Pepper 66
Stuffed Eggs and Tomato
  67
Stuffed Peppers 68
Sunday Breakfast 69
Super Curried Eggs
  Indian Style 70
Swiss Fondue 71
Swiss Schnitzel 72
Swiss Steaklets 73
Teriyaki 74
Tomato Pie 75
Tomato Rice 76
Tomato Soufflé 77
Tomatoes Provençal and
  Mince 98
Vegetable Burger Stew
  with Tomatoes, Peas
  and Cheese Topping 99
Vegetable Burger
  Supreme 100
Vegetable Burgers in
  White Wine 101
Vegetable Curry 102
Vegetables and Baked
  Schnitzels in White
  Wine 103